Lecture Notes in Computer Scier

Commenced Publication in 1973
Founding and Former Series Editors:
Gerhard Goos, Juris Hartmanis, and Jan van Leeuwen

Sonja Klingert   Xavier Hesselbach-Serra
Maria Perez Ortega   Giovanni Giuliani (Eds.)

Energy-Efficient Data Centers

Second International Workshop, E^{2}DC 2013
Berkeley, CA, USA, May 21, 2013
Revised Selected Papers

 Springer

Volume Editors

Sonja Klingert
University of Mannheim
Software Engineering Group
Mannheim, Germany
E-mail: klingert@informatik.uni-mannheim.de

Xavier Hesselbach-Serra
Technical University of Catalonia (UPC)
Barcelona, Spain
E-mail: xavier.hesselbach@entel.upc.edu

Maria Perez Ortega
GFI Informática
Madrid, Spain
E-mail: mportega@gfi.es

Giovanni Giuliani
HP Italy Innovation Center
Cernusco sul Naviglio, Milano, Italy
E-mail: guiliani@hp.com

ISSN 0302-9743   e-ISSN 1611-3349
ISBN 978-3-642-55148-2   e-ISBN 978-3-642-55149-9
DOI 10.1007/978-3-642-55149-9
Springer Heidelberg New York Dordrecht London

Library of Congress Control Number: 2014937553

LNCS Sublibrary: SL 2 – Programming and Software Engineering

Typesetting: Camera-ready by author, data conversion by Scientific Publishing Services, Chennai, India

Printed on acid-free paper

Springer is part of Springer Science+Business Media (www.springer.com)

Preface

In 2010 the number of computers finally exceeded the number of human users, and the current trend will result in approximately 14 machines per on-line user by 2020[1]. This computing power is primarily concentrated in huge server farms and other data centers that, world-wide, consume roughly 300 TWh of electricity[2]. Even though the efficiency of each IT service is increasing, the overall trend in energy consumption is inexorably heading in one direction: upwards!

As one of the major energy consumer groups, data centers must therefore contribute significantly to the goal of reducing global CO_2 emissions by a factor of 10 by 2050 in order to avoid drastic climate changes. This can be accomplished through innovative technologies and processes either within the data center itself or in collaboration with end-users and/or the electricity supply system. To promote such solutions, we continued the E^2DC workshop series started in 2013 with the Second International Workshop on Energy-Efficient Data Centers, E^2DC 2013, focusing both on energy-aware data center technologies and the role of data centers in the global energy system. The workshop was collocated with the ACM SIGCOMM e-Energy 2013 conference in Berkeley, California, on May 21, 2013, and organized by the EU FP7 project All4Green[3].

These proceedings of the workshop cover a wide range of relevant technologies from information and communication technologies for green data centers to business models and GreenSLAs, as well as the collaboration between data centers and energy providers in order to avoid costly power peaks and/or to integrate renewable energy sources.

The first part of the proceedings contains three papers in the context of energy and workload measurement. Z. Abbasi et al. evaluated the impact of workload and renewable prediction on geographical workload and energy buffering management. They showed through a simulation study, using realistic traces, that the proposed method, with and without prediction error, is effective in reducing average energy cost and increasing sustainability of data centers. The problem of controlling the applications' workload in renewable energy-aware data centers was challenged by C. Dupont in a second contribution, aimed at fostering a better utilization of renewable energy in data centers. The next presentation by M.T. Beck et al. tackled the estimation of photo-voltaic power supply without smart metering infrastructure, by means of models suited for small-scale areas in a small-scale power grid. These models can be used by energy providers to

---

[1] George Slessman, "End of Life – Data Centre 1.0.", talk at Data Centres Europe, 2013

[2] http://www.tech-pundit.com/wp-content/uploads/2013/07/Cloud_Begins_With_Coal.pdf?c761ac

[3] www.all4green-project.eu

determine the power available from photovoltaic power plants (state estimation) that are not directly connected to the communication infrastructure.

In the second part, dealing with energy management issues, a proposal for an energy-aware database management was presented by C. Bunse et al., showing that software has a significant impact on the energy consumption of a system and demonstrating that high-performance algorithms often require more energy than slower ones. In the last talk of this session, J. F. Botero et al. proposed a novel data center control architecture for power consumption reduction, providing a high-level view of the modules and functionalities required for achieving the collaboration between the actors of the eco-system.

The third session analyzed simulators and control approaches. M.V. Berge et al. suggested a model for data center efficiency building blocks used in energy-efficiency and thermal simulations, showing how these models are affected by specific architectures of modeled hardware and differences between various classes of applications. T. Bostoen et al. introduced a simulator to assess energy-saving techniques in content distribution networks, targeting energy savings in these networks, including the analysis of the HTTP-adaptive-streaming workload from an operational content distribution network delivering IPTV. In the last paper, S. Janacek showed results from a data center smart grid integration study considering renewable energies and waste heat usage, to obtain the best possible synergy effects between the data center and the smart grid in terms of energy exchange and infrastructure usage.

There were 38 attendees, nearly half of whom came from the USA, China, and India and half from Europe: Finland, Belgium, Poland, Germany, Italy, and Spain. The workshop also included four additional presentations: The keynote was given by Mary Ann Piette (Lawrence Berkeley National Laboratory) who spoke about the automation of demand response and communication systems. Maria Perez Ortega (GFI) and Sonja Klingert (University of Mannheim) explained the common approach of the EU projects FIT4Green and All4Green: FIT4Green aimed at learning to control the energy consumption in data centers through an energy-aware plug-in to the data center management system; All4Green now uses this control for demand response schemes with energy providers. The management of energy data was the focus of the talk by Audrey Lee (California Public Utilities Commission); and finally the presentation by Christos Kolias (Orange Silicon Valley) addressed software-defined networking and network function virtualization in energy-efficient data centers. G. Ghatikar gave further insights into how to expand data center energy efficiency objectives through integration into the smart grid by using demand response approaches.

The final item on the agenda was a discussion panel: Chaired by Hermann de Meer (University of Passau) and Jorjeta Jetcheva (Fujitsu Labs of America), Rolf Bienert (OpenADR Alliance), Nada Golmie (NIST), Tedd Sheffer (CAISO), Bernhard Thies (VDE/VDI), Girish Ghatikar (LBNL), and Dennis Symanski (EPRI) conducted a lively discussion on "Data Center Challenges, Standards landscape, and the Future Requirements."

We would like to thank all authors for their contributions to these proceedings and in particular the reviewers for their hard work in evaluating the submissions. This significantly helped to improve the initial submissions and made our work easier when selecting the papers. We would also like to thank all volunteers who dedicated their talent and time to the workshop organization: Special thanks are due to the e-Energy 2013 organizers, especially to Catherine Rosenberg (University of Waterloo) and Hermann de Meer (University of Passau) for their continuing support and the generously provided opportunity to collocate the workshop with ACM SIGCOMM e-Energy 2013, to Jorjeta Jetcheva (Fujitsu Labs of America) who helped organize the panel, and to Springer LNCS for organizational support in preparing the proceedings.

Finally, we are grateful for the strong support from the European Commission and the ICT FP7 All4Green project.

July 2013   Sonja Klingert
Xavier Hesselbach-Serra
Giovanni Giuliani
Maria Perez-Ortega

Organization

Workshop Chairs

Sonja Klingert   University of Mannheim, Germany
Xavier Hesselbach-Serra   Universitat Politècnica de Catalunya, Spain

Organization Chairs

Maria Perez Ortega   GFI, Spain
Giovanni Giuliani   HP Innovation Center, Italy

Technical Program Committee

Colin Atkinson   University of Mannheim, Germany
Robert Basmadjian   University of Passau, Germany
Christian Bunse   University of Applied Sciences Stralsund,
     Germany
Ivona Brandic   Vienna University of Technology, Austria
Marta Chinnici   ENEA, Italy
Ron Doyle   IBM, USA
Daniel Gmach   HPLabs, USA
Erol Gelenbe   Imperial College London, UK
Jorjeta Jetcheva   Fujitsu Laboratories of America, USA
Thierry Klein   Alcatel-Lucent, USA
Bastian Koller   HLRS, Germany
Barbara Pernici   Politecnico di Milano, Italy
David Snelling   Fujitsu Laboratories Europe, UK
Tuan Anh Trinh   Budapest University of Technology
     and Economics, Hungary
Wolfgang Ziegler   SCAI Fraunhofer, Germany

Sponsoring Institutions

EU FP7 Project All4Green (#288674)
University of Mannheim, Germany
Universitat Politècnica de Catalunya, Spain
GFI, Spain
HP Innovation Center, Italy

Table of Contents

Impact of Workload and Renewable Prediction on the Value of Geographical Workload Management*

Zahra Abbasi, Madhurima Pore, and Sandeep K.S. Gupta

Impact Laboratory,
School of Computing, Informatics and Decision Systems Engineering,
Arizona State University
Firstname.Lastname@asu.edu

Abstract. There has been increasing demand for energy sustainable and low-cost operation in cloud computing. This paper proposes dynamic Geographical Load Balancing and energy buffering management (GLB) to achieve these goals which (i) shifts workload (particularly peak workload demand) toward Data centers that offer low utility rate or green energy at a time, and (ii) banks excess green and low-cost energy to shift peak workload demand away from high utility rate. Such a scheme needs to be aware of the workload intensity and the available renewable power of the cloud in future (over a relatively long prediction window such as a day). Existing solutions mainly focus on developing algorithms and demonstrating the cost efficiency of GLB, disregarding the prediction accuracy of the workload and the renewable power. However, erroneous information decreases the efficiency of GLB. This paper studies the performance of the online GLB solution when using time-series based prediction techniques (e.g., ARIMA) for the workload and the renewable power (i.e., solar and wind). The results of the simulation study using realistic traces highlight that GLB with and without prediction error is effective in reducing average energy cost and increasing sustainability of data centers. Further, GLB is shown to be significantly effective in shaving peak power draw from the grid (e.g., reducing peak power upto 100%), however the erroneous information due to the prediction error adversely affects its performance. Furthermore, the simulation study indicates that the optimal mix of the renewable power (i.e., wind and solar) to be leveraged by GLB, is achieved when data centers are powered from both the solar and the wind power.

Keywords: Cloud computing, Data Centers, Workload Prediction, Renewable power, electricity cost, Energy Storage, Energy Management.

1 Introduction

Data center power consumption is raising concerns to both operators and society due to its huge electricity cost, scalability and detrimental impact on the environment. Particularly, there has been increasing push toward using renewable power in data centers from environmental activist [1, 2]. Large-scale Internet service providers, such as

---

* This work has been partly funded by NSF CRI grant #0855527, CNS grant #0834797, CNS grant #1218505 and Intel Corp.

S. Klingert et al. (Eds.): E²DC 2013, LNCS 8343, pp. 1–15, 2014.

Google, Microsoft and Yahoo! and other modern data centers have begun to partially power their data centers using on-site and other offline forms of the renewable energy resources [3, 4].

Recent works propose that dynamic Global/Geographical Workload Balancing (GLB) can potentially be a significant aid in maximizing renewable energy utilization and reducing energy cost without need for large scale Energy Storage Devices (ESDs) [5–12]. The idea is to leverage spatio-temporal variation of the workload, the renewable power and the electricity power to match the demand with low-cost and green power supply. However, the potential benefits of such a scheme have been a point of debate in the community [10,11,13]. On one hand, it is clear that, due to spatio-temporal variation of power supply and demand across data centers, GLB creates many energy management possibilities to lower electricity price, lower energy consumption, and efficiently manage the renewables [5–12]. On the other hand, there are also significant costs for its implementation in practice. These costs come in terms of the engineering challenges in implementing and designing efficient and automated algorithms. Fortunately, *cloud computing*, facilitating a dynamic, demand-driven allocation of computation, allows workload distribution across data centers. Additionally, the algorithmic challenges, in terms of time-efficiency, and making online decisions on workload distributions and energy buffering without requiring the knowledge of the future workload has been studied in literature [8, 12, 14]. Despite this body of the work, the question of characterizing the potential benefits of GLB has still not been properly addressed. Particularly, the proposed online algorithms, are based on simplification assumptions on the data center workload type [12], energy supply models and energy management objectives [8, 12, 14]. Also, it is shown that the efficiency of some of online solutions compared to the optimal offline solution depends on the prediction window length [13]. However, the existing solutions mainly rely on the predictability of data and ignore the possible impact of the prediction error on the performance of the algorithm. The predictability of input data is partially true, since some of the information, i.e., workload, electricity price, solar energy are shown to have nice cyclic behavior, and are thusly predictable. However, wind energy does not exhibit cyclic behavior and is thusly hard to predict. Also, generally, the prediction accuracy decreases with increasing the prediction window length. This raises concern that prediction error might be a significant downgrading factor on the efficiency of the global workload management.

Further, recent literature propose to utilize ESDs to shave the peak power draw from the grid, as it significantly contributes in the total electricity price of data centers [15, 16]. The idea is to use ESDs to smooth out the power draw from the grid. In this paper, we propose a comprehensive solution to integrate GLB with energy buffering management in order to shave peak power draw from the grid. Spatio-temporal variation of workload allows GLB to further smoothen the power draw from the grid. This necessitates an online workload management scheme with forecasting knowledge over a relatively long time in future [17].

Furthermore, recent works demonstrate that the wind energy is more valuable than the solar energy for Internet-scale systems, to be leveraged by global workload management [10, 18]. The reason is that the wind energy has little correlation across locations, and is available during both night and day. This suggests that the optimal renewable

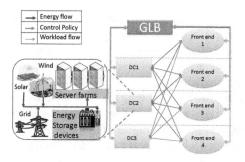

Fig. 1. GLB system model

energy mix of the wind and the solar leveraged by GLB is dominated by the wind power. However, such a result is only true if we assume that the wind and the solar energy are perfectly predictable. We study such an effect in this paper.

In summary our main contribution is to study a workload management that that co-ordinately manages the workload, energy buffering, and peak power draw of a cloud though an analytical model and illustrate its efficiency in presence of erroneous information of the workload, and the available renewable energy due to their prediction error. Our trace-based simulation study show that:

- GLB with and without prediction error yields higher renewable energy utilization (up to 20% for GLB with zero prediction error and up to 10% for GLB with prediction error) and consequently lower energy cost (up to 60% for GLB with zero prediction error and up to 50% for GLB with prediction error) compared to a conventional performance oriented load balancing scheme.
- The optimal renewable energy mix of the solar and the wind energy for GLB: (i) to increase the renewable utilization is achieved when both the wind and the solar energy contribute in the total renewable energy, (ii) to increase the GLB cost saving by reducing the impact of prediction error is achieved when there is more solar energy than wind energy.
- GLB when using forecast data increases the peak power draw from AC up to two times compared to when it accesses accurate data. These results are *pessimistic* since the values are compared to a baseline load balancing scheme which (i) manages local ESDs within data centers to shave peak power draw, and (ii) relies on the perfect knowledge of the workload and the renewables.

2   GLB System Model and Formal Definition

Our simulation experiments combine analytical models with real traces for workload and renewable availability, to allow controlled experimentation but provide realistic findings. We now explain the system model and formulation of online GLB which extends the model presented in [6] to include energy buffering and to account the electricity cost per peak power draw from the grid.

GLB for interactive jobs can be generally modeled as a network flow optimization model on a bipartite graph (see Fig. 1). End users' requests arrive from $|A|$ geographically distributed front-ends (i.e., the sources) where $A = \{a_1 \ldots a_j \ldots a_{|A|}\}$ denotes the set of front-ends. The geographical front-ends may be network prefixes, or even geographic groupings (states and cities).

The workload must be distributed among the $|S|$ available data centers in the cloud (i.e., sink), where $S = \{s_i\}, i = 1, \ldots, |S|$ denotes the set of available data centers in the cloud, and each s_i represents the total number of available servers in data center i. Also data centers may be provided with an energy storage of limited size, B^{size}, to smoothen renewable as much as possible.

There are many possible energy optimizations that can be developed considering various combination of factors such as workload split of data centers, power state of servers, migration of user state data, energy buffering level and performance level of applications. For simplicity, we only focus on the workload split, a two power state for servers (active and off), renewable harvesting and energy buffering. The goal is to perform workload consolidation over minimal number of servers in the most cost-efficient data center at a time. Extra servers are assumed to be turned off. GLB performs the optimization in a time-stepped system where the time is discretized into intervals, slots, and over a window of time intervals, denoted by T. We consider one hour slots for a window of a day. At the start we present mathematical modeling of GLB consisting energy consumption, cost, performance, workload, ESDs, and renewable energy models.

Table 1. Symbols and Definitions

Symbol	Definition	Symbol	Definition
t	slot index	γ_i	cost per charging/discharging
i	index of data centers	B_i^{size}	energy storage capacity
j	index of areas	ρ_i	energy loss coefficient
S	set of data centers	$\alpha_{i,t}$	cost per average power draw from the grid
A	set of front ends (areas)	β_i	cost per peak power draw from the grid
T	Prediction window length	η	carbon footprint cap
τ	length of slots (in second)	f_i	function of DC's power consumption
$p_{i,t}^{ESD}$	charging (for a positive value) and discharging (for a negative value)	$y_{i,t}$	number of active servers
		μ_i	service rate
$p^{max,discharge}$	maximum discharging rate	$\lambda_{j,t}$	workload arrival rate
$p^{max,charge}$	maximum charging rate	d_i'	data center delay
p^{AC}	power draw from grid	$d_{i,j,t}''$	delay between areas and
$p^{total}{}_{i,t}$	total power consumption		data centers
$r^{total}_{i,t}$	average available green power	d^{ref}	total reference delay
$r_{i,t}$	renewable harvesting	d'^{ref}	service delay

Performance Modeling. We assume that delay experienced by a user, denoted by d should not exceed a reference delay, denoted by d^{ref}. Total delay, d, consists of the service delay d', i.e., data center delay, and the network delay d'', i.e., the delay between the front-end and the data center. As a result, the delay can be written as $d = d' + d''$. We model data center as a M/M/n queuing system and use its result to model service delay. We assume a time-varying delay between every front-end j and data center i to model the network delay.

Workload Modeling. We model workload through its statistical parameters, i.e., average arrival rate and service time over every slot. Let $\lambda_{j,t}$ denote the mean arrival rate from front-end j at time t. To provide realistic estimates, we use real-world traces to denote $\lambda_{j,t}$. We consider four front-ends, corresponding to four time-zones in USA. We generate the workload of each front-end using NASA workload Internet data center trace (July and August, 1995) [19], such that it is shifted in time to account for time zone of each front-end, and scaled proportionally to the number of Internet users in the corresponding area (see Fig 2).

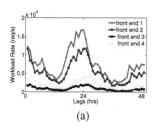
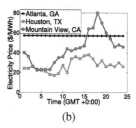

(a)   (b)

Fig. 2. (a)NASA workload [19] scaled and shifted according to time zone for each front end, and (b) Hourly electricity price data for three locations on May 2nd, 2009 (data source [5])

Energy Consumption Modeling. We assume the total power consumption of the data center can be obtained by multiplying the total number of active servers (denoted by y) and power consumption value for each server (denoted by p). To keep the optimization framework linear, we set p as the power consumption of servers when they are utilized at their peak utilization.

ESD Modeling. We assume ESDs are associated with physical limitations on their size, B^{size}, measured in Joule, maximum charging discharging rate denoted by $p^{max,discharge}$, and $p^{max,charge}$, and energy efficiency (due to conversion) denoted by ρ. To account for the ESD cost we account the limits of the discharging cycles and state the capital cost of an ESD in terms of every discharge cycle. We denote such a cost as γ which incurs every discharging cycle. To model energy storage, we denote the energy storage level at time t by B_t with initial value B_0 and the charge/discharge at time t by p_i^{ESD}, where positive or negative values mean charge or discharge, respectively.

Renewable Energy Modeling. We assume wind and solar energy as sources of renewable energy located on-site in a data center. To capture the availability of wind and solar energy, we use traces of [20]. We use wind speed and the rated power to calculate the wind power, and Global Horizontal Irradiance (GHI) and the ambient temperature to calculate the solar power using models described in [9]. The traces of three states for three days are illustrated in Fig 3. We scale the traces to study the efficiency of GLB under various configuration of the available renewable power.

GLB Cost Model. We consider an electricity pricing model to account for both the electricity cost per average energy consumption, $\alpha_{i,t}$ (see Fig. 2(b)), and β_i per excess peak power draw from stipulated power (denoted by p_0) over a month. The later is used

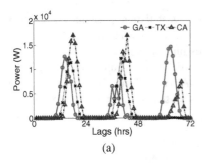 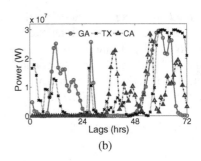

| (a) | (b) |

Fig. 3. Data traces showing variation of renewable energy generated at the three data center locations [20]: **(a)** Trace for solar energy, and **(b)** Trace for Wind energy

Minimize
$$\sum_{i=1}^{|S|} \left(\sum_{t=1}^{T} \left(p_{i,t}^{AC} \tau \alpha_{i,t} + b_{i,t} \gamma_i \right) + \max_{1 \le t \le T} (p_{i,t}^{AC} - p_0)^+ \beta_i' \right),$$

subject to:

[ESD const.] , $\forall\, t, i$: $r_{i,t} + p_{i,t}^{AC} = p_{i,t}^{total} + p_{i,t}^{ESD}$,

$B_{i,t+1} = \min(\eta_1 (B_{i,t} + \rho_1 p_{i,t}^{ESD} \tau), B_i^{max})$,

$-b_{1,t} p_i^{max,discharge} \le p_{1,t}^{ESD}$,

$0 \le b_{i,t} \le 1, r_{i,t} \le r_{i,t}^{total}$,

$p_{i,t}^{ESD} \le p_i^{max,discharge}$,

$-p_{i,t}^{ESD} \le p_1^{max,discharge}$.

[Capacity const.] , $\forall\, t, i$: $p_{i,t}^{total} = p_i y_{i,t}, \; y_{i,t} \le s_i$.

[Service const.] , $\forall\, t, j,$: $\sum_{i=1}^{|S|} \lambda_{i,j,t} = \lambda_{j,t}$.

[Queuing const.] , $\forall\, t, i$: $y_{i,t} \mu_t \ge \sum_{j=1}^{|A|} \lambda_{i,j,t}$.

[Delay const.] , $\forall\, t, i$: $d'^{ref} \le \frac{1}{\mu} + \frac{1}{y_t \mu - \lambda_t}, d_{i,j,t} = d_i'^{ref} + d_{i,j,t}'', \; (d^{ref} - d_{i,j,t}) \lambda_{i,j,t} \ge 0$.

Fig. 4. Linear Programming (LP) formulation of GLB problem

to penalize the peak power draw from the utility. Note that we consider a prediction window of length T for GLB problem that is less than a month. However, to use GLB to smooth the peak power, we incur a fraction of β, i.e., $\beta' = T\beta$/number of slots in a month per excess peak power during T, to penalize peak power draw. A solution to this problem would specify, at each slot, how many servers in each data center should be assigned to the workload (i.e., $y_{i,t}$), what portion of each front-end's traffic should be assigned to which data center (i.e., $\lambda_{i,j,t}$), and how much is average power draw from AC, (i.e., $p_{i,t}^{AC}$), renewable (i.e., $r_{i,t}$), and energy storage (i.e., $p_{i,t}^{ESD}$, and $B_{i,t}$). We approximate $y_{i,t}$ as a real and solve this problem as a linear programming model. Cost minimization is subject to the following constraints:

– *ESD constraint* which asserts the power demand and supply balance, energy level of ESDs over time which is affected by its charging/discharging (p^{ESD}), its energy efficiency, ρ, and its self-discharge ratio, η, and battery cost that is incurred per each discharging cycle using a linear approximation equation.

- *Service constraint* which asserts that all workload should be assigned to the data centers.
- *Capacity constraint* i.e., the number of assigned active servers in a data center should not exceed the available servers (denoted by s_i) in that data center. Further, each data center should supply power required for all of its active servers.
- *Queuing stability constraint* which asserts the M/M/n stability condition.
- *Delay constraint* i.e., the traffic of end users should be split among data centers whose network and service delay is less than the users' delay requirement.

3   GLB Solution Using Prediction

In our solution, we evaluate the efficiency of the schemes by forecasting workload and renewable using time-series prediction methods (i.e., SARIMA and moving average) and the well known Rolling Horizon Control (RHC) technique. Consider a window of length T, RHC obtains GLB solutions at time t by solving the cost optimization over the window $(t, t + T)$, given the GLB solution at time $t - 1$. The following sections discuss the workload and the renewable energy prediction (i.e., predicting $\lambda_{i,t}$, and $r_{i,t}^{total}$ over the window $t + T$) and their results. Note that the electricity price, i.e. α is usually known a day ahead [11], further electricity price, workload, and solar energy have daily variations. For that we choose the prediction window of a day (24 slots), and assume the actual electricity price is given for the entire window.

3.1   Workload Prediction

We analyze NASA workload using different time series based prediction techniques and observe that Seasonal ARIMA (Auto Regressive Integrated Moving Average) captures the seasonal behavior of workload (see Fig. 2) with reasonable accuracy (compared to non-seasonal schemes). We use the workload data for the month of July of NASA trace for learning the SARIMA model, and use the trace of August in our numerical analysis. For every time slot, using workload information known up to that time slot, we forecast for the next 24 hours using the prediction model. For time slot of 1 hour we observe prediction error of 25.8% that increases up to 42.6% for higher lags as shown in Fig. 5(a).

3.2   Renewable Power Prediction

We use sample traces from the solar and wind energy sites in Georgia (GA), Texas (TX) and California (CA) for the months of February and March [20].

3.2.1   Solar Energy Prediction
The variation in solar power shows a daily seasonal behavior as seen in Fig. 3(a). This pattern is captured by SARIMA. For learning SARIMA model we use one month trace

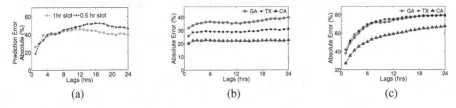

Fig. 5. Prediction error plots for different lags as obtained for 24 hours of forecast window **(a)** Workload, **(b)** Solar power, and **(c)** Wind power

of February. The model is fitted by changing the parameters to minimize the error observed in the residual plots and the ACF and PACF (Auto Correlation and Partial Auto Correlation) plots. Predicted solar energy for one week is shown in Fig. 3. The error for different lags is almost constant starting with 23% for TX, and up to 25% for GA. The error obtained for different lags for prediction is shown in Fig. 5(b).

3.2.2 Wind Energy Prediction
The wind power shows a highly varying nature which depends on different factors, such as temperature, pressure, wind directions(see Fig. 3(b)). Hence prediction of wind using seasonal time series prediction is not so effective. We use the moving average technique to predict the wind energy. We observe that the average error for a given forecast window increases rapidly with increasing the prediction window length, starting with 30% for window of length one (hour) and increasing up to 80% for a window of length 24 (a day). Comparing Figs. 5(b) and (c), demonstrating the prediction error of solar and wind energy for different lags, we observe that the wind energy incurs much higher prediction error for lags greater than one than that of the solar energy.

4   Simulation Study

4.1   Data Center Setup

We simulate a cloud consisting of three data centers as depicted in Fig. 1. The electricity pricing and physical characteristics, such as server power profiles, battery of data centers are set according to realistic data. To this end, we assume data centers are located at the following three locations: Atlanta, GA; Houston, TX; and Mountain View, CA, namely DC1, DC2 and DC3, respectively. These locations correspond to the location of three major Google data centers. We used the historical electricity prices for the above locations [5] (see Fig. 2(b)) as example in our setup. We perform experiments for both homogeneous and heterogeneous setting of data centers in terms of their servers' power efficiency as depicted in Table. 2. We assume each server can handle upto 2000 requests and that there is no network delay. The data sheet of Fload Lead Acidic (FLA) batteries used in data centers is used for simulation study (see Table 3). We also assume each data center have 500 servers, and the workload intensity in our experiment is such that 600 active servers are needed on average. Our simulation environment is developed

Table 2. Data center characteristics

DC	Elec. price model	peak power(W)
DC1	Mountain View, CA.	395
DC2	Houston, TX	300
DC3	Atlanta, GA	450

Table 3. Specification of ESD parameters

Parameters	FLA
Capacity (KW)	115
Cost per discharge ($)	0.65
Cycle life of one cell (cycles)	1200
Discharge rate (W)	5387.5
Discharge-to-charge ratio	10
Efficiency (%)	80
Number of cells	53

using MATLAB 2009. We use GNU Linear Programming Kit (GLPK) to solve GLB (i.e., optimization problem in Fig. 4).

4.2 Experiments Performed

We design **Performance-oriented Load Balancing (PLB)** as a baseline scheme, which distributes workload equally across all data centers. For fair comparison, we assume PLB utilizes ESDs and determines number of active servers to optimize cost within each data center independently (i.e., solving problem in Fig. 4 for each data center). To evaluate the impact of prediction error on the efficiency of GLB we compare **GLB when using Perfect Prediction (GLB+PP)** with GLB when using our prediction technique (GLB+P). Note that GLB+PP accesses actual data over every prediction window of T. *Similarly, to characterize the maximum impact of the prediction error we assume that PLB accesses the actual data over every prediction window to perform energy buffering management in each individual data center*, in reality PLB also needs to predict the data, though. We evaluate the above schemes in terms of energy and ESD cost (i.e. the two first items in the objective function of Eq. 4), excess peak power draw from the grid, total energy consumption and renewable utilization with various cloud configuration (e.g., ESD size, and available renewable energy). To calculates peak power draw over a month, the stipulated power is set to 80KW, ($p_0 = 80kW$) a value that is 60% more than average power consumption of our simulated data center.

Available Renewable Energy. We set the original renewable (wind+solar) traces such that the solar and the wind power contribute equally in the total renewable energy of

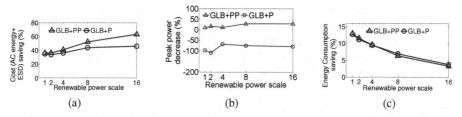

Fig. 6. Efficiency of GLB compared to PLB versus renewable power increase; **(a)** energy and ESD cost saving, **(b)** Peak power draw decrease, and **(c)** Total energy consumption decrease

data centers. Further, the renewable energy contributes 10% of the cloud total energy consumption. Then we scale the renewable traces from 1-16 as depicted in Fig. 6 to evaluate the efficiency of GLB with increasing availability of the renewable energy. We also set the ESD capacity to 12MJ for each data center, a value that is equivalent to the energy consumption of data centers for one minute when operating at their peak. Finally, we use a heterogeneous setting of data centers (see Table 2).

Fig. 6(a) shows that both GLB+PP and GLB+P outperform PLB in terms of energy and ESD cost. However, prediction error negatively affects the GLB cost saving, causing a decrease in cost saving from 60% for GLB+PP, down to 45% for GLB+P. Further, while the cost saving of GLB+PP increases with increase in the available renewable energy, this is not the case for GLB+P.

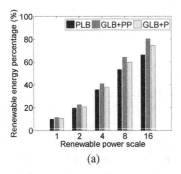
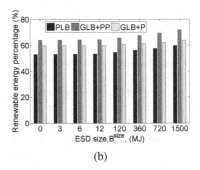

(a)   (b)

Fig. 7. (a) Renewable energy percentage of total energy versus increase in available renewable energy, and **(b)** Renewable energy percentage of total energy versus increase in ESD size

The results of Fig. 6(b) imply that the effect of prediction error is huge for peak power draw, as GLB+P increases the peak power draw from the grid up to 2 times compared to PLB that accesses a perfect prediction scheme. In reality, both PLB and GLB need to predict data. GLB+PP, however, significantly decreases the peak power compared to PLB. Particularly, it decreases the peak power (compared to PLB) from 10% up to 40% with increasing renewable energy.

Fig. 6(c), shows that both GLB+PP and GLB+P decrease the total energy consumption of the cloud compared to PLB, that is due to shifting workload to DC2 which has lesser peak power per server (see Table. 2). The figure shows that GLB+P has higher energy consumption saving than that of GLB+PP, this is because GLB+PP does not highly utilize DC2 to decrease its peak power. The energy saving decreases with increasing the available renewable, since GLB schemes shift the workload towards data centers that have more available renewable energy instead of shifting the workload to data centers that have more power efficient servers.

Finally, Fig. 7 (a) shows that both GLB+PP and GLB+P increase the utilization of the renewable energy compared to PLB.

ESD Capacity. In this experiment we scale the renewable power by the factor of eight, use heterogeneous setting of data centers (see Table 2), and vary ESD capacity from 0 up to 1500MJ, where 1500MJ is equivalent to the energy consumption of data centers for two hours when operating at their peak. Fig. 8(a) shows that both GLB schemes, i.e., with and without prediction error, induce lesser cost than PLB for zero size ESD capacity. The cost saving of GLB+P decreases with increasing ESD size, since PLB can leverage ESD to utilize low-utility rate electricity. This implies that by decreasing the opportunities for GLB to leverage spatio-temporal variation of renewable and low-cost electricity compared to workload management within data centers (in this case due to deploying large scale ESD in each data center), the impact of prediction error on downgrading the performance of GLB becomes higher.

Similar to Fig. 6(b), Fig. 8(b) shows that GLB+P increases the peak power up to 2 times compared to PLB. This is because PLB by using accurate data can shave the peak power using local ESD. However, the same figure shows that GLB+PP can decrease the peak power up to almost two times depending on the ESD size, compared to PLB. This result shows the value of GLB in shaving peak power draw from the grid when it uses an accurate prediction technique. Finally, Fig. 7 (b) shows that both GLB+PP and GLB+P increase the utilization of the renewable energy compared to PLB. However, the renewable utilization of GLB+PP increases with increasing ESD size, that is not the case for GLB+P.

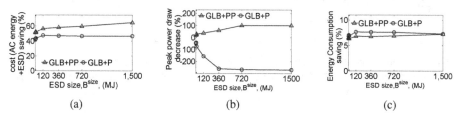

Fig. 8. Efficiency of GLB compared to PLB versus ESD capacity increase; **(a)** energy and ESD cost saving, **(b)** Peak power decrease, and **(c)** Total energy consumption decrease

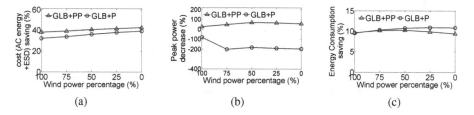

Fig. 9. Efficiency of GLB compared to PLB versus various mix of wind and solar; **(a)** Energy and ESD cost saving, **(b)** Peak power decrease, and **(c)** Total energy consumption decrease

Wind and Solar Energy Mix. In this experiment, we fix the renewable scale to the factor of 8, ESD capacity to 360MJ (an energy storage for each data center to work for 30 minutes with server working at peak utilization), and use a heterogeneous setting of data centers. We vary the contribution of the wind power from 100% down to 0%.

The results shown in Fig. 9 indicate that the cost saving and energy saving of GLB schemes increase with increasing solar energy contribution. This means that PLB can not highly utilize excess solar energy with a relative high ESD size, since the solar energy is only available during the days. However GLB schemes, can leverage the spatio-temporal variation of the available renewable energy and efficiently utilize it. Interestingly, the cost saving of GLB+P increases with increasing the solar energy contribution, that is partly due to less prediction error of the solar energy compared to the wind energy (compare Fig. 5(b) and (c)). Finally, Fig. 10 (a) shows that the highest utilization of renewable for all schemes is achieved when there is a mix of both the wind and the solar (70-50% wind power), since with this mix, renewable power is almost available at all the time.

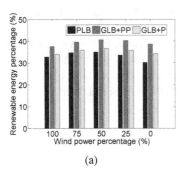
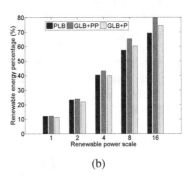

(a)   (b)

Fig. 10. (a) Renewable energy percentage of total energy consumption versus various mix of wind and solar energy, and **(b)** Renewable energy percentage of total energy for homogeneous DCs versus increase in available renewable

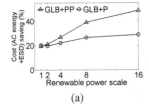
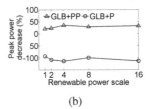
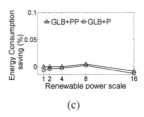

(a)   (b)   (c)

Fig. 11. Efficiency of GLB compared to PLB for homogeneous setting of data centers **(a)** energy and ESD cost saving, **(b)** Peak power draw decrease, and **(c)** Total energy consumption decrease

Homogeneous Data Centers. We repeat the first experiment for the homogeneous setting of data centers where all data center consume 300W at peak per each server. Fig. 11 shows that for the homogeneous setting of data centers, GLB schemes can significantly save cost due to leveraging electricity price variation and available renewable across the cloud. Peak power draw plot (i.e., Fig.11(b)) has the same trend as that of (i.e., Fig.6(b)). Fig.11(c) shows that GLB schemes slightly (around 0.0005%) increase the energy consumption compared to PLB, that is because the GLB schemes increase ESD utilization and consequently its energy loss. Comparing Fig. 10(b), with Fig. 7(a) indicates that the renewable utilization trend of GLB+PP and PLB is the same. However,

GLB+P does not always incur higher renewable utilization than that of PLB, confirming the previous results that when there is lower opportunity to leverage power and cost efficiency (in this case homogeneous setup of data centers), the impact of prediction error in decreasing the performance of GLB worsens.

4.3 Discussion

In summary, the above results show that, with the presence of erroneous information, the GLB scheme is still more effective in maximizing the utilization of renewable energy compared to the conventional performance oriented load balancing scheme (i.e., PLB). Particularly, it leverages spatio-temporal variation of power efficiency, power cost, and renewable in reducing energy cost, and increasing the renewable utilization without requiring a large-scale energy storage. However, pessimistically GLB with prediction error (GLB+P) increases the peak power drawn from AC compared to PLB with zero prediction error. Since peak power cost may be significant in some data centers, these results necessitate the need for developing: (i) online algorithms that can shave the peak power without having knowledge about the future, and (ii) prediction techniques to predict workload and renewable energy with very low prediction error.

The above results, however, heavily depend on the prediction accuracy. Although we do not claim superior performance of SARIMA over the other prediction techniques, it is a fairly stable and frequently used in the literature, particularly, for Internet workload prediction [7, 18, 21]. Further, we observe a prediction error that is very similar to what is reported by the previous works (for lag one prediction) [18, 22]. The prediction of renewable energy particularly for small window length and relatively short time intervals (e.g., one hour) can be improved using weather forecast data, however such approaches tend to be inaccurate at medium time scales (e.g., three hours to one week) [23].

5   Related Work

Similar to our results, related works highlight that global workload management can significantly reduce the electricity bill [5, 6, 8, 11, 12], and can potentially reduce the carbon footprint of data centers without requiring large-scale ESDs [7, 9, 10, 24, 25]. However, the focus of the above work are either demonstrating the efficiency of such a scheme using numerical study, or developing efficient algorithms. Particularly, Qureshi et al perform numerical analysis to show the efficiency of GLB on reducing the electricity price [11]. Le et al. demonstrate the carbon footprint reduction of the cloud using global workload management [7]. Akoush et al. and Stewart et al. show that workload management across data centers can increase the utilization of renewable [24, 25].

The algorithmic issues of GLB are studied in some recent literatures [5, 6, 8]. These literature assume a proactive and a time-stepped system for the scheme, where the workload intensity is assumed to be predicted ahead of time. However, the impact of the prediction error is not sufficiently studied. As such [18] proposes a cooling and renewable aware workload management within data centers. The authors use a regression based predictor and k-nearest classification to predict workload and solar power, respectively. Similar to our result, they report an average error of 20% for both workload and solar power (for lag one). The authors show that the prediction error of data has negligible effect on the optimality of the solution. However, we show that when using a large prediction window, the impact of prediction error on shaving peak power is huge.

GLB when integrated with energy buffering management [14], workload migration overhead [6, 12], or server switching cost [13] can only be optimally solved using an offline algorithm. Accordingly, some online algorithms with guaranteed competitive ratio are proposed [12–14]. Particularly, Lin et al., derive a competitive ratio (i.e., online optimal solution over the offline optimal solution) and prove that the competitive ratio decreases with increasing the prediction window length. However, our results show that the prediction error increases with increasing the prediction window length (see Fig. 5). [14] proposes an online algorithm to utilize ESDs in order to leverage temporal variation of energy cost in data centers. However, more recent work propose to shave peak power draw using ESDs, since it is a big contributor of total electricity cost in data centers [15, 16]. Shaving peak power draw from grid requires an online workload management algorithm which uses forecast data for a relatively long window length [17]. Our results show that GLB is very effective in shaving peak power draw when it uses accurate data. However, erroneous information adversely affects its performance.

6   Conclusion

This paper proposed global workload management (GLB) integrated with energy buffering to increase renewable utilization, reduce average energy and peak power cost across data centers. The paper studied online GLB solution using SARIMA technique to predict the workload and the renewable energy over a window (i.e., 24 hours). The trace-based simulation study, shows that GLB with and without prediction error (i.e., GLB+P and GLB+PP) outperform over the performance oriented-load balancing, PLB, in increasing renewable energy utilization and reducing energy cost. The results are pessimistic since PLB is assumed to access accurate data as opposed to GLB+P. Results also highlight that GLB needs an accurate predictor to enable shaving peak power draw from the grid. Such prediction accuracy is not achieved using SARIMA based prediction, necessitating future work to design accurate prediction techniques.

References

1. Clancy, H.: Facebook becomes renewable energy activist website,
   http://www.zdnet.com/blog/green/facebook-becomes-renewable-energy-activist/19656 (cited January 2013)
2. greenpeace.org, Greenpeace activists project messages on apple headquarters from supporters asking for cleaner cloud (cited January 2013)
3. Demasi, G.: More renewable energy for our data centers,
   http://googleblog.blogspot.com.ar/2012/09/more-renewable-energy-for-our-data.html (cited January 2013)
4. Mcmillan, R.: Apple vows to build 100% renewable energy data center,
   http://www.wired.com/wiredenterprise/2012/04/applerenewable/ (cited January 2013)
5. Rao, L., Liu, X., Xie, L., Liu, W.: Minimizing electricity cost: optimization of distributed Internet data centers in a multi-electricity-market environment. In: Proc. IEEE INFOCOM, pp. 1–9 (2010)

6. Abbasi, Z., Mukherjee, T., Varsamopoulos, G., Gupta, S.K.S.: DAHM: A green and dynamic web application hosting manager across geographically distributed data centers. ACM Journal on Emerging Technology (JETC) 8(4), 34:1–34:22 (2012)

7. Le, K., Bilgir, O., Bianchini, R., Martonosi, M., Nguyen, T.D.: Managing the cost, energy consumption, and carbon footprint of internet services. In: Proc. of ACM SIGMETRICS, pp. 357–358 (2010)

8. Liu, Z., Lin, M., Wierman, A., Low, S.H., Andrew, L.L.H.: Greening geographical load balancing. In: Proc. ACM SIGMETRICS, San Jose, USA, June

9. Zhang, Y., Wang, Y., Wang, X.: Greenware: Greening cloud-scale data centers to maximize the use of renewable energy. In: Kon, F., Kermarrec, A.-M. (eds.) Middleware 2011. LNCS, vol. 7049, pp. 143–164. Springer, Heidelberg (2011)

10. Liu, Z., Lin, M., Wierman, A., Low, S.H., Andrew, L.L.H.: Geographical load balancing with renewables. ACM SIGMETRICS Perf. Eval. Rev. 39(3), 62–66 (2011)

11. Qureshi, A., Weber, R., Balakrishnan, H., Guttag, J., Maggs, B.: Cutting the electric bill for Internet-scale systems. In: Proc. ACM SIGCOMM, pp. 123–134 (2009)

12. Buchbinder, N., Jain, N., Menache, I.: Online job-migration for reducing the electricity bill in the cloud. In: Domingo-Pascual, J., Manzoni, P., Palazzo, S., Pont, A., Scoglio, C. (eds.) NETWORKING 2011, Part I. LNCS, vol. 6640, pp. 172–185. Springer, Heidelberg (2011)

13. Lin, M., Liu, Z., Wierman, A., Andrew, L.L.H.: Online algorithms for geographical load balancing. In: Proc. of IEEE IGCC. IEEE (June 2012)

14. Urgaonkar, R., Urgaonkar, B., Neely, M.J., Sivasubramanian, A.: Optimal power cost management using stored energy in data centers. In: Proc. of ACM SIGMETRICS, pp. 221–232 (2011)

15. Wang, D., Ren, C., Sivasubramaniam, A., Urgaonkar, B., Fathy, H.: Energy storage in datacenters: what, where, and how much? In: Proc. of the 12th ACM SIGMETRICS, pp. 187–198 (2012)

16. Kontorinis, V., Zhang, L.E., Aksanli, B., Sampson, J., Homayoun, H., Pettis, E., Tullsen, D.M., Rosing, T.S.: Managing distributed UPS energy for effective power capping in data centers. In: Proc. of the 39th IEEE ISCA, pp. 488–499 (2012)

17. Bar-Noy, A., Johnson, M.P., Liu, O.: Peak shaving through resource buffering. In: Bampis, E., Skutella, M. (eds.) WAOA 2008. LNCS, vol. 5426, pp. 147–159. Springer, Heidelberg (2009)

18. Liu, Z., Chen, Y., Bash, C., Wierman, A., Gmach, D., Wang, Z., Marwah, M., Hyser, C.: Renewable and cooling aware workload management for sustainable data centers. In: Proc. of the 12th ACM SIGMETRICS, pp. 175–186 (2012)

19. http://ita.ee.lbl.gov/html/traces.html

20. NREL, Measurement and instrumentation data center MIDC, http://www.nrel.gov/midc/

21. Jung, G., Hiltunen, M.A., Joshi, K.R., Schlichting, R.D., Pu, C.: Mistral: Dynamically managing power, performance, and adaptation cost in cloud infrastructures. In: Proc. of 30th IEEE International Distributed Computing Systems (ICDCS)

22. Goiri, Í., Beauchea, R., Le, K., Nguyen, T.D., Haque, M.E., Guitart, J., Torres, J., Bianchini, R.: GreenSlot: scheduling energy consumption in green datacenters. In: Proc. of 2011 International Conference for High Performance Computing, Networking, Storage and Analysis, pp. 20:1–20:11 (2011)

23. Sharma, N., Gummeson, J., Irwin, D., Shenoy, P.: Cloudy computing: Leveraging weather forecasts in energy harvesting sensor systems. In: Proc. of 7th Annual IEEE Conference on Sensor Mesh and Ad Hoc Communications and Networks (SECON), pp. 1–9 (2010)

24. Stewart, C., Shen, K.: Some joules are more precious than others: Managing renewable energy in the datacenter. In: Workshop on Power Aware Computing and Systems (2009)

25. Akoush, S., Sohan, R., Rice, A., Moore, A.W., Hopper, A.: Free lunch: Exploiting renewable energy for computing. In: Proceedings of HotOS (2011)

Renewable Energy Aware Data Centres: The Problem of Controlling the Applications Workload

Corentin Dupont

University of Trento
Trento, Italy
corentin.dupont@unitn.it

Abstract. Data centres are powerful facilities which aim at hosting ICT services. They have huge needs in term of power supply; furthermore the current trend is to prioritize the utilization of renewable energies over brown energies. Renewable energies tend to be very variable in time (e.g. solar energy), and thus renewable energy aware algorithms tries to schedule the applications running in the data centres accordingly. However, one of the main problems is that most of the time very little information is known about the applications running in data centres. More specifically, we need to have more information about the current and planned workload of an application, and the tolerance of that application to have its workload rescheduled. In this paper, we will first survey the problem of understanding, building information about and finally controlling the load generated by applications. Secondly we will propose hints of solutions for that problem.

Keywords: Data Centre, Renewable Energy, Application Profile, Resource Management, Job Scheduling.

1 Introduction

In the last decade, energy-awareness has been of great concern for researchers. Indeed, the prices for electricity are constantly getting higher and carbon emissions to the environment are increasing every year[1]. Users try to switch off the lights or put the ICT devices in sleep mode when not needed. This straightforward approach works fine for domestic appliances but more complicated ICT facilities like data centres (DCs) require, however, more sophisticated approaches to achieve the energy savings while preserving the performance. Data centres are large facilities which purpose is to host information processing and telecommunication services for scientific and/or business applications. Until recently, research on data centres has been focused only on improving metrics like performance, reliability, and availability. However, due to the rise in service demands together with energy costs, the energy efficiency has now been added as a new key metric for data centres. Energy-aware strategies are beginning to be integrated inside the data centre resource manager. In practice, a

---

[1] Green Grid Consortium, http://www.thegreengrid.org

S. Klingert et al. (Eds.): E²DC 2013, LNCS 8343, pp. 16–24, 2014.

Virtual Machine (VM) placement algorithm considers the data centre and the workload characteristics to place the VMs among the servers in the most efficient way, considering performance and energy consumption. This placement must be done respecting the requirements of the Service Level Agreement (SLA) existing between the data centre and its clients.

In parallel to reducing the overall energy consumption, the current trend is to foster the use of renewable energies. Renewable energies have the problem to be very variable and time-dependent: for example solar power is available only during the day, and is subject to variations due to the meteorological conditions. Thus, renewable energy aware algorithms in data centres must try to shift the workload of running applications in time, to match it with the availability (or forecasted availability) of renewable energy. This is however difficult because generally very little information is known about a running application. It is thus necessary to augment this "meta" knowledge about applications running in data centres, to allow better match-making between green energy availability and the requirement of the applications in term of energy. Secondly, having provided this meta-data, the applications must provide a way for the data centre management framework to control, at least partially, the workload to be run. In this paper we survey the problem of understanding and controlling the workload of applications, with the final objective to allow energy aware algorithms to perform better energy savings.

In the remainder of this paper, we will first perform a survey of the related works in section 2 and define the problem that need to be solved in Section 3. We will then propose a possible solution architecture and technologies in Section 4 and finally conclude in Section 5.

2   State of the Art

The problem described is transversal: it is spanning several domains such as energy aware algorithms, data centre management systems, application profiling and static property derivation from applications. We review the related works in two sub-sections: the optimization algorithms frequently used in Data Centres and how they are embedded in data centre management frameworks in a first part, and then we will survey existing techniques on automatic program property derivation, and specifically of the application profile.

2.1   Energy Aware Optimization Algorithms in DC Management Frameworks

Virtualization was and still is the main feature for saving energy in data centres. It allows to right-size the largest culprits of energy over-consumption which are underutilized servers. In typical environments these machines sit idle almost all of the time and consume a significant amount of energy that is not needed in practice to satisfy the requirements of the applications. In a virtualized data centre, applications are embedded into virtual machines (VMs) that are consolidated on a reduced amount to servers to increase their utilization then lower the overall energy utilization. In addition, live migration allows re-arranging the VMs placement without significant disruption to the underlying services, to be able to react to fluctuating resources requirements. There is an abundant literature on energy aware algorithms for data centres. To lower the energy consumption while fulfilling performance requirements, the authors of [1] propose a flexible and energy-aware framework for the (re)allocation of virtual machines (VMs) in a data centre. The framework, being independent from the data centre management system, computes and enacts an energy aware placement of virtual machines based on constraints expressed through service level agreements (SLA). This problem is known to be NP-hard [2] with a large solution space. The framework's flexibility is achieved by decoupling the expressed constraints from the algorithms using the Constraint Programming paradigm and programming language. The problem of consolidating and rearranging the allocation of virtual machines in a data centre in an energy efficient manner is described in [3]. In the heuristic proposed in [3], the algorithm computes, for each VM to be moved, the appropriate hosting server that leads to minimizing the current overall power consumption of a data centre. This is similar to the First Fit Decreasing (FFD) algorithm which has been used in previous works [4][5], with the addition of power-awareness for choosing the server. The limitation of these frameworks comes from the fact that it has only a macroscopic view of the "size" of the workloads, which is often mapped to the reserved size of the VMs. For example, Amazon EC3 defines only a few VM size (i.e. M1 small, M1 medium...). This prevents a fine consolidation of the VMs, as resources have to be reserved for each instance.

2.2   Advanced Distributed Computing Paradigms

Hadoop[2] is a very popular open source solution for distributing workload across multiple nodes, implementing the MapReduce [6] paradigm. In this paradigm, a computation over a set of data is broken into a "map" function and a "reduce" function. The map function can be performed simultaneously and independently over different sub-sets of data. This independence of the computations allows for massive distribution of the computation on many computers. In a second step, the result of the map functions is collected and the final result is computed by the reduce function. GreenHadoop [7] uses Hadoop as a data-processing framework, and makes prediction about the availability of solar power. These predictions are used to schedule time-bound computations in order to maximize the green energy consumption of the data centre. However, Hadoop and the solutions based on it have an inherent limitation: the computations must be expressed in term of a map and a reduce functions, which is a great constraint. This is a very restrictive programming paradigm and furthermore not every computation can be expressed in such a way. GreenSlot [8] tries to schedule jobs in Supercomputing data centres in order to maximize the use of renewable energy. It uses historical data and weather forecasts to determine the best moment of day to run a particular job. However, GreenHadoop and GreenSlot suffer from the fact that, in both case, the user have to describe the workload/job characteristics

---

[2] Hadoop: http://hadoop.apache.org/

(notably its time-bound constraints). This information is at best very coarse grained, and sometime not available at all.

Still in the domain of distributed computing, the newly introduced serializable delimited continuations of Scala may allow to overcome the limitations of MapReduce. Scala is a general purpose programming language designed to express common programming patterns in a concise, elegant, and type-safe way. It smoothly integrates features of object-oriented and functional languages. Swarm[3] is a framework for Scala allowing the creation of applications which can scale transparently through the continuation-based approach mentioned before. Like Map-Reduce, Swarm follows the maxim "move the computation, not the data". Swarm takes the concept much further, allowing it to be applied to almost any computation, not just those that can be broken down into map and reduce operations. However, Swarm is still at a very early stage. A "GreenSwarm", taking into account renewable energy availability in a way akin to that of GreenHadoop, would undoubtedly be an interesting development for this technology. In the same line of thinking, Cloud Haskell [9] is a domain-specific language (DSL) for distributed computing developed in Haskell (a purely functional general purpose language). It also uses serialized function closures for transmitting computations across the network.

As already mentioned before, Amazon Elastic Compute Cloud (EC2) is defining several sizes of VMs that their clients can pick up. However this level of granularity does not allow a fine consolidation of the VMs, and does not give a lot of information on the profile of the applications running, and specifically their planned variation of load in time. The building of an application (or workload) profile is addressed briefly in [10]. Historical values are used to consolidate a profile for the workload. However, no standard is described allowing the transmission and reuse of this profile. It would be of course very interesting to build this application profile automatically or semi-automatically, for example by analysing the source code of the application. Property derivation from programs and property proving is very close to theorem checking in mathematics: there is a one to one correspondence between a program and a proof (called the Curry-Howard correspondence). In [11], the authors implement a tool called HipSpec able to automatically derive and prove properties of functional programs.

3   The Problem: How to Understand the Load of Applications?

A great challenge of using efficiently renewable energies in data centres is to be able to schedule correctly the applications workload. Indeed, as shown on Figure 1, the availability of renewable energy can have a great variation in time, with comparison to brown energies. To increase the use of renewable energies with respect to brown energies, it is necessary to shift in time the workload of some applications in the data centre. This shows the importance of being able to know the workload an application will have to run at a certain point of time, to understand under what conditions it can be shifted or delayed, and *in fine* to schedule it correctly.

---

[3] Swarm: http://www.scala-lang.org/node/3485

Scheduling ~50% Renewables   Scheduling ~90% Renewables

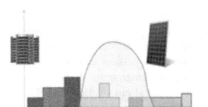 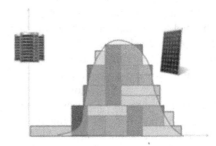

Fig. 1. Matching the application workload with the availability of the renewable energies

Yet, currently most of the applications running in data centres are unaware of their self workload: they are unable to predict how much computing power they will require and when. Furthermore, the time scale at which computational workload in data centres vary can be very different from the time scale at which renewable energy may vary. For example, renewable energies may have seasonal variations, like solar energy availability, while load in data centres can have short timed variations, like hourly or daily variations.

It is of crucial importance for many ICT domains to be able to know what an algorithm contained in an application will need in term of computing resources, and yet there are little developments in this field. In data centres, the knowledge of the requirements of an application in terms of resources is still "meta-knowledge", i.e. the knowledge of the data centre operators. It is the role of the data centre operator to provision sufficient resources for an application, and this provision is often done in a static way. For example, in data centres, database indexing maintenance operations are usually performed at night, to minimize the impact on the overall performance. However, in a data centre using primarily solar power, it would be interesting to shift this task during the lunch break, when the sun is shining. The knowledge that this particular task, "database indexing", can cope with a 12 hour shift, and that it takes approximately half an hour, belongs to the operator's knowledge. It is very coarse grained and subjective knowledge.

The optimization algorithms used in data centres typically needs to know the profile of applications in order to minimize a utility function (for example the energy consumption). A heuristic widely used for data centre VM management is bin-repacking, and among meta-heuristics we can count Constraint Programming, Genetic Algorithm or Simulated Annealing. For example a multi-dimensional bin-repacking will help consolidate the VMs on a part of the servers and permit switching off another part of the servers, thus saving energy. However this algorithm needs to know the profile of the applications in term of memory consumption and CPU demand in order to map those parameters to the abstract dimensions of the objects to be packed.

This advocate the need for:

    1)   a standardized format and protocol for applications to advertise in real-time their own needs in term of resources, including possible performance

trade-offs and uncertainty ranges (this format is part of the so-called "application profile"),

2) a library and programming methodology to ease the extraction of application profiles from the application source code itself, at run-time or compile-time,

3) a data centre management framework and algorithms able to read the application profiles and use them to consolidate and schedule the applications on the servers in the appropriate way, in order to minimize a given utility function,

4) a library and programming methodology to allow an external process to control the application load to some extent.

The problem of deriving an application profile is very accurate in many load optimization and prediction problems. More generally, automatic derivation of program macroscopic properties is a topic that has a great number of applications in the ICT field, especially with the emergence of Cloud computing. For example, a smart phone application might want to "off-load" part of its workload to the Cloud, or on the contrary, a service running in the Cloud might be relocated in the local device for performance reasons. These application or service migrations must be controlled by a decision framework, which must know the exact applications profile in order to take the right migrations decisions.

We need to research and develop the algorithms, methodologies and tools to make applications "self aware" to a certain extent. In practice very seldom applications are able to know "what" workload they have to perform and when it needs to be done. They just "do it", in some sense. There is no internal representation of this workload, or when there is one (like in Hadoop or some database management framework), it is not general enough and standardized.

4   A Possible Architecture

We present an architecture for the communication between the different actors of a data centre producing and using the application profile.

In Figure 2, the DC authority can force the DC management framework to respect some energy consumption limitations and give possible trade-offs in term of performance. At the same time the renewable energy producer will give details on the energy mix available, and the forecasts for the next days. The DC management framework will then collect the application profiles from the running applications. The DC management framework will ask to the applications, according to the information contained in these profiles, to respect some load conditions and time restrictions in order to globally match the workload of the data centre with current and forecasted renewable energy availability. Additionally, at a more macroscopic level the traditional VM and server management can happen: VMs can be migrated in order to consolidate them on a part of the servers and the freed off servers can be switched off to save energy.

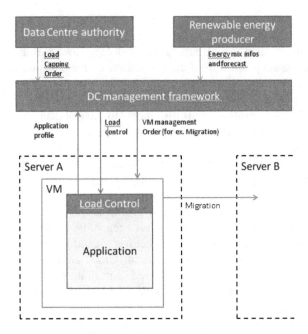

Fig. 2. Architecture overview

4.1   Representing the Application Workload

Applications running on desktop operating systems (for ex. Linux, Windows or Mac OS) typically communicate very few to no information to their host operating system when launched. For example, a multi-threaded application will ask the creation of its threads to the operating system, thus letting it know the number of threads. The idea is to increase this amount of information in the case of applications running in data centres, to let the operating system and subsequently the data centre management framework build an appropriate and up to date application profile. Based on this profile, the load balancer and scheduling system of the data centre will be able to make better optimizations of the workload.

The granularity of the virtualization in a Cloud data centre is at the level of the Operating System: the Virtual Machines are containing one OS, and this is what is benchmarked and possibly moved. This level is still macroscopic: usually a server contains around 10 VMs. However, the hosted OS may contain many applications. Better energy savings could possibly be achieved if this level of granularity was lower. We also need a way to let the application externalize some of its workload. A bit like in Hadoop, the application could let to an external process the task to distribute and run a part of its workload. Recent advances in parallel processing may let us perform efficient workload allocation (see Section 2). If the application embeds its own scheduler and doesn't externalize its workload, it should nevertheless be able to receive orders or advises on the best moments to run its workload from the DC management framework. In that respect, currently, the applications offer very little cooperation with the operating system. In multi-task systems, the application will let the OS pre-empt it. But it will not let the OS know if a computationally intensive activity needs to be done mandatorily in the next hour, for example.

The applications need to be more "self-aware": they need to have an internal representation of their own processes and workload. In other terms, they need to know "what" they have to do, and not just "how" to do it. As already mentioned before, applications are usually working in a "procedural" way: they describe a step by step method to solve a problem, but do not have a more macroscopic representation of this problem. The idea is to include in the application profile what the applications need to do and when, to a certain extend and with a certain granularity. For example, in the case of the application indexing a database, the application needs to "know" that this process can be delayed, and needs to transmit that to the DC Management System.

4.2   Extracting the Application Profiles

To extract automatically the application profile, a possibility is to perform static analysis of the application source code itself in order to infer the complexity of the algorithms. This is in the general case impossible to perform mechanically, because of theoretical limitations (namely the indecidability of the halting problem [12]). However, the general idea would be to provide a library to allow the programmer to "instrument" the code with meta-data about the various algorithms complexity. This meta-data would be composable, in the same way that simple algorithms may be composed to build a more complex algorithm. This would allow retrieving, at a higher level, the complexity of algorithms and giving hints on the maximum and average resources needed by the application. This information will be collected by the management framework of the data centre and allow fine-grained allocation and optimization, using the optimization algorithms mentioned before.

A second way one could establish dynamic properties of programs, is to use a theorem prover. With such a tool, a programmer could bundle his program with the proof that certain properties such as a maximum load hold true. Proving properties of programs is much easier in functional programming because it is semantically simpler than imperative programming and thus, easier to reason about.

5   Conclusion

In this paper we presented the problem that faces the algorithms aiming at fostering a better utilization of renewable energy in data centres: the lack of information about the running applications at a macroscopic level. We need a way to automatically or semi-automatically derive an application profile, to collect it and exploit it at data centre level, with the aim to allow renewable energy algorithms to perform better. Indeed those application profiles are necessary as an input for optimization methods typically used in data centres. The information contained in the application profile will be used to compute the allocation and scheduling of the applications. We presented a possible architecture and technologies able to create this application profile, to transmit it to the data centre management framework, and finally to control accordingly the applications workload in order to better utilize renewable energies.

Acknowledgments. The authors would like to thanks the reviewers for their useful comments.

References

[1]   Dupont, C., Giuliani, G., Hermenier, F., Schulze, T., Somov, A.: An energy aware framework for virtual machine placement in cloud federated data centres. In: Proceedings of the Third International Conference of Future Energy Systems: Where Energy, Computing and Communication Meet, e-Energy (May 2012)

[2]   Lawler, E.: Recent results in the theory of machine scheduling. In: Mathematical Programming: The State of the Art. Springer, Berlin (1983)

[3]   Quan, D.-M., Basmadjian, R., De Meer, H., Lent, R., Mahmoodi, T., Sannelli, D., Mezza, F., Dupont, C.: Energy efficient resource allocation strategy for cloud data centres. In: Proceedings of the 26th International Symposium on Computer and Information Sciences, ISCIS 2011, London, UK, September 26-28, pp. 133–141. Springer (2011)

[4]   Bobroff, N., Kochut, A., Beaty, K.: Dynamic placement of virtual machines for managing SLA violations. In: 10th IFIP/IEEE International Symposium on Integrated Network Management, IM 2007, pp. 119–128 (May 2007)

[5]   Wood, T., Shenoy, P.J., Venkataramani, A., Yousif, M.S.: Black-box and gray-box strategies for virtual machine migration. In: Proceedings of the 4th ACM/USENIX Symposium on Networked Systems Design and Implementation, Cambridge, MA, USA, p. 17. USENIX Association, Berkeley, CA (2007)

[6]   MapReduce: Simplified Data Processing on Large Clusters, Jeffrey Dean and Sanjay Ghemawat

[7]   Goiri, I., Le Thu, K., Nguyen, D., Guitart, J., Torres, J., Bianchini, R.: GreenHadoop: Leveraging Green Energy in Data-Processing Frameworks.

[8]   Goiri, et al.: GreenSlot: Scheduling Energy Consumption in Green Datacenters. In: Supercomputing (2011)

[9]   Epstein, J., Black, A.P., Peyton-Jones, S.: Towards Haskell in the Cloud

[10] Talaber, R., et al.: Using Virtualization to Improve Data Centre Efficiency, The Green Grid consortium (2009)

[11] Claessen, K., Johansson, M., Smallbone, N., Rosen, D.: HipSpec: Automating Inductive Proofs of Program Properties

[12] http://www.princeton.edu/~achaney/tmve/wiki100k/docs/Halting_problem.html

Estimating Photo-Voltaic Power Supply without Smart Metering Infrastructure

Michael Till Beck[1,3], Hermann de Meer[1],
Stefan Schuster[2], and Martin Kreuzer[2]

[1] Computer Networks and Communications, University of Passau, Germany
{michael.beck,hermann.demeer}@uni-passau.de
[2] Symbolic Computation, University of Passau, Germany
{stefan.schuster,martin.kreuzer}@uni-passau.de
[3] Stadtwerke Passau GmbH, Passau, Germany

Abstract. Due to the lack of appropriate grid communication infrastructure, many energy providers can only measure a very limited subset of their PV plants and therefore have only limited knowledge of the power flow inside their grid. Existing approaches to estimate the total amount of PV energy produced at present time ("nowcasting") require external data such as sun radiation or temperature that are often not available online. Using approximate computational algebra, we construct polynomial models to derive grid-specific formulae estimating the PV power provisioning without the need of additional data. We evaluate our approach based on real data from a German energy provider and demonstrate the accuracy of the derived models. Besides nowcasting, two additional application scenarios, snapshot provisioning and simulation of power flow, are discussed.

1 Introduction

Recently, many European countries integrate huge amounts of renewable based power sources into the grid. They intend to reduce dependencies on fossil sources like coal, oil, and nuclear resources. Some countries like Germany, Italy, and Belgium even aim at completely eliminating these dependencies on nuclear power. In many other European countries political ambitions are similar, since many countries now bolster the integration and utilization of renewables and debate nuclear power phase-outs.

Mainly driven by political objectives, the amount of renewable energy sources that are fed into the power grid heavily increased in Germany lately. The German government advocates the integration of renewable based power generation in favor of reducing dependencies on nuclear power sources. In 2011, the German government announced their objective to shut down all German nuclear power stations by 2022. For this reason, large arrays of wind turbines and solar panels have been installed. In addition to that, the German government assured monetary incentives to citizens that install photo-voltaic panels on their residence's roof. Most of these private power plants are rather small in size and only produce a limited amount of power. However, many citizens decided to participate

S. Klingert et al. (Eds.): E²DC 2013, LNCS 8343, pp. 25–39, 2014.

in the initiative due to monetary incentives granted. So in total, across Germany, photo-voltaic power production rapidly increased (and is still continuously increasing) within the power grid.

Traditionally, the power grid was not intended to cope with the integration of large amounts of highly fluctuating energy sources. Therefore, the main challenge with power plants that are based on renewables like wind or solar radiation is that power production is highly fluctuating and, in general, hard to predict. Fluctuations, however, directly influence and destabilize the frequency in the grid, if the energy provider can not cope with them in terms of adapting its other power plants in-time or (with respect to demand/response mechanisms) negotiating with flexible customers. In this case, the energy provider has to fall back to (negative or positive) balancing reserve power which comes with very high costs. For these reasons, precise prediction of energy that is expected to be available in the (near) future is essential for the energy provider due to economical and ecological reasons.

Photo-voltaic power generation is drastically increasing in Germany. During the year 2010, approximately 7 GWpeak of solar power plants were installed, which, at that time, rapidly increased the total available capacity by 70%. Power generated by these new photo-voltaic power plants was often underestimated by the distribution system operators (DSOs). In Germany, this became most conspicuous in September 2010, where an unexpected imbalance of +7 GW occurred for several hours. The German DSOs were not able to predict this rapidly increasing amount of positive imbalance, as they underestimated the impact of the newly installed panels. Thus, adaption of their power plants could not be performed in time. Since overproduction exceeded all of the available negative balancing reserve power (4300 MW), a huge amount (∼2800 MW) had to be paid to other countries. This resulted in high costs and almost in a break down of the grid [1] [2].

The reason for these kinds of underestimations lies in the current infrastructure of the grid. Energy providers just have started to upgrade grid infrastructure. This includes, but is not limited to additional power lines and communication channels. In almost every part of Germany (and also in many other European countries), smart metering devices have not yet been deployed due to excessive additional expenses and efforts. This also means that most of the photo-voltaic panels can not be measured directly. In fact, approximately 75% of a total of 900.000 photo-voltaic power plants can not be measured directly due to technical limitations [2].

Therefore, in the age of renewable energy sources, energy providers have to monitor grid stability, e.g., by estimating the amount of power provided by the photo-voltaic plants that can not be measured directly. Being able to obtain more accurate information, energy providers can react more precisely to discrepancies, which leads to an increase in overall, trans-regional grid stability.

In this paper, we introduce a novel nowcasting methodology to estimate the total available photo-voltaic power by mathematically analyzing correlations of power provisioning characteristics. In contrast to others, our approach does not depend on external information like solar radiation or additional information on the type and alignment of panels. Therefore, our approach is expected to be more accurate, especially in regional contexts. Furthermore, we are confident that accuracy of existing forecasting algorithms can be significantly improved by also taking into account the hidden interdependencies of PV plants. This is especially interesting for demand/response mechanisms that are subject of current research: Instead of just tailoring energy provisioning to the demand, demand/response mechanisms are currently also integrated into grid infrastructures: In case of power shortages/surplus, energy demand of flexible customers can be reduced by notifying them to adapt power consumption accordingly. Up to now, demand/response mechanisms have been deployed for major customers like big factories only, since they show the most potential of power adaption capabilities.

However, current research also focuses on integrating mid-size consumers like data centres into the grid (or even small customers like private homes)[3][1]. Since data centres are expected to be able to adapt power demand much more fine-grained than factories, more accurate information of power surplus/shortage is becoming more and more important. Using nowcasting techniques, a *snapshot* of the current state of the grid can be derived, which is a valuable input for these adaption mechanisms.

We run our evaluation on data provided by an energy provider located in Bavaria, Germany. First results show that the approach seems to be quite promising, even for small-scale grids and small geographical distances between power plants.

2   Background

The integration of renewable power sources into traditional power grids comes with several difficulties and challenges, since they notably differ from traditional, fossil based power sources. During the day, power quality needs to be maintained in the grid continuously for the grid to remain stable. High power quality means that voltage and frequency do not (or only within very tight boundaries) vary from specific values. Disruptions and disturbances caused by unforeseen effects have to be avoided by all means to ensure that power provisioning is working properly and to avoid grid failure [4]. Traditionally, this has to be ensured by the responsible energy provider by switching off unneeded power plants in time in case there is additional power fed into the grid by renewable power sources. Similarly, the energy provider has to react timely if these additional power sources disappear. A major challenge in this respect is that adapting these "'traditional"' power sources has to be done quickly, i.e., as fast as the renewables appear or

---

[1] The All4Green project, which is funded by the European Union, aims at integrating data centres into the smart grid. It introduces new service level agreements for data centres (and also for its end users) to define the degree of flexibility in terms of quality of service. For further information, please refer to http://www.all4green-project.eu

disappear. Therefore, energy providers have to carefully plan ahead hours of operation of their power plants, since provisioned power has to match demands.

For this reason, energy providers have to take weather forecasts into account, which introduce uncertainties in terms of predictability. Predictability, however, is of significant importance for the energy provider for operating economically and ecologically. Power that is provided by various kinds of power plants always relies on constraints that come with these differing power plants and the power sources they use. For example, due to technical reasons, several models of diesel generators can only be used for a limited number of times a year; nuclear power plants can not provide power immediately after they are switched on. Thus, in general, there are four types of power plants that distinguish in reactiveness, ecologic footprint, and economic costs:

1. Base Load Power Plants:
   Power plants delivering high amounts of inflexible energy. They are inflexible in terms of reactiveness, but power provisioning in general is relatively cheap. These power plants can not be used to cover Medium Load, nor can they compensate quickly fluctuating power sources.
   Examples: nuclear power plants, coal power plants

2. Medium Load Power Plants:
   These power plants can react quicker than Base Load Power Plants to changing demands. I.e., they can cover the lack of energy that was forecasted to be provided by a photo-voltaic plant if the changed weather conditions were predicted hours or several minutes before. However, Medium Load Power Plants can not be used to cover on-demand events.
   Examples: combined gas and steam energy generators

3. Peak Load Power Plants:
   Peak Load Power Plants react quickly and almost in-time to unforeseen changes. However, the usage of these plants is costly and in general also involves high CO2 emissions.
   Examples: diesel generators and gas turbines

4. Plants relying on uncontrollable power sources:
   Power plants that are not controllable in terms of power provisioning times. These power plants depend on renewable energy sources like sun or wind. Since these sources are highly fluctuating and their local availability and disappearance are hard to predict, huge amounts of additional power might rapidly disappear in the grid, so the energy provider has to adapt power provisioning of its other plants in-time. Weather forecasting techniques are an essential tool for reasonable, economically arrangement.

Thus, grid stability is a complex task, and power demands and power supply have to be planned carefully. For this reason, the European grid is not just a collection of individual, national (or even local) grids, but is highly interconnected.

This allows to transfer cheap energy (that is currently available in the south of Europe, for example) to the north, if it is not needed. In general, this also helps to stabilize the grid, since partners can help compensating local instabilities. I.e., a local energy provider is connected to its preceded energy provider. The preceded provider might also provide a major contribution to the energy supplied locally, usually within stipulated bounds.

As a consequence of integrating fluctuating renewable sources like solar power plants and wind turbines, energy providers have to cope with two main challenges: Power Shortage and Power Surplus.

1. Power Shortage

   Power shortage is often caused by special mainstream events (e.g., football matches), changing weather conditions (sudden drop of renewable energy due to upcoming, sky-covering clouds or reduced wind), or due to seasonal conditions (e.g., heating in winter, usage of air-conditioning during summer months). To cover power shortages, economically and ecologically expensive peak load power generation has to be activated, or additional power needs to be bought from third-party suppliers (that might even reside in a foreign country). Otherwise, the grid will become unstable and break down.

   Basically, there are two reasons for a power shortage: Failures or forecast deviations. In case of a power plant's breakdown, power supply suddenly drops within the grid and other plants have to compensate the lack of power generation. The same happens if there are forecast deviations, i.e., if forecasted reneable based energy generation differs significantly from their real power supply. Figure 1a depicts a shortage at 12pm. The maximum amount of power supplied from the preceded energy provider exceeds the stipulated bounds and the lack of power can not be compensated by own power plants.

2. Power Surplus

   If more power is available than demanded, the energy provider has to deal with power surplus. This can be caused by sudden increases of uncontrollable

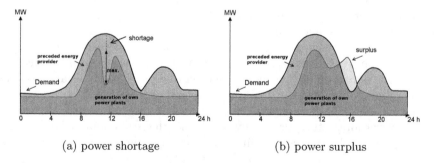

(a) power shortage   (b) power surplus

Fig. 1. Deviations of power supply and power demand

power plants (e.g., wind and no clouds) or the fact that power demand is decreasing (e.g., on sunny Sundays or holidays, where industrial production is paused and people go outside). In this case, power plants have to be switched off (either completely or partly). Sometimes, unneeded power resources even have to be sold to third party suppliers/foreign countries, mostly with negative prices. Otherwise, a power surplus will lead to grid instability.

Reasons for a power surplus are similar to the ones described for power shortages: One reason is that there are failures, i.e., on the side of a (big) customer. In this case, power demand suddenly decreases and power plants have to be adapted accordingly. Another reason is that there might be deviations from forecasts so that power plants could not be arranged accordingly in time. Figure 1b depicts a surplus of energy: At around 4pm, there is more energy generated by, e.g., solar power plants than needed.

3   Related Work

Up to now, research has investigated in two closely related, but still different areas in this field: *Forecasting* and *Nowcasting* techniques. Forecasting aims at predicting the available amount of power provisioning that will be available in the future. Based on weather forecasts, energy providers can estimate how much energy will probably be available within the next couple of hours (or even days). Then, based on this information, they can derive how much additional energy they have to buy from third party suppliers or on the stock market – or, in case of a power surplus, how much energy they have to sell.

Therefore, prediction methods are used for estimating the demanded amount of power. In this case, forecasting mostly focuses on inter-day predictions, i.e., on expected weather conditions for the next day, or even on intra-day to predict weather changes within the next few hours. However, from the energy provider's perspective, short-term forecasting techniques are getting more and more attractive. This is mainly due to the rapid integration of photo-voltaic panels in several parts of Europe. Weather forecasting is highly complex and, therefore, prediction of available energy is very error prone in this case. Especially, forecasting of direct sunlight beam is much more inaccurately to perform than global irradiance. Several approaches have been proposed to predict future weather conditions. Also, based on weather forecasting, several methods have been introduced to estimate the actual amount of power that will be provided by solar panels or wind turbines. [5] evaluates and compares several of them.

In general, since both forecasting approaches (weather forecasting, and, based on this, power forecasting) are highly unreliable, the real amount of power provided by renewable sources can differ significantly from the predicted values. Several Demand/Response protocols like OpenADR guarantee incentives to the customers that are willing to support the energy provider by adapting their power consumption accordingly. These incentives should be based on the current state of the grid, i.e., power consumption that needs to be decreased/increased. However, in many European countries like Germany, grid infrastructure is not ready for the integration of a more complex communication system, i.e., Smart Metering. Therefore, the real amount of currently available photo-voltaic power can not be determined exactly, since measurement data can not be sent to the energy provider. Therefore, Saint-Drenan et al. propose a novel approach to estimate the amount of photo-voltaic power based on sattelite data [2].

In this paper, we propose another nowcasting approach to detect hidden dependencies derived solely from a subset of photo-voltaic power plants. We aim to provide a methodology to derive models that are accurate even for small-scale grids and small geographical distances.

4   Estimating Available Photo-Voltaic Supply in the Grid

We aim at deriving grid-specific formulae to estimate the amount of power fed into the grid by power plants that can not be measured continuously. The approach currently used by German energy providers to estimate this amount assumes a linear relation to the amount of energy which is produced by a small number of directly measured PV plants [6]. However, as discussed in [2], the situation is more complicated: Due to certain characteristics of PV plants (e.g., module orientation) the correlation of produced PV energy between different PV plants is in general rather low. Assuming not linear but more generally *polynomial* relations between PV plants, we therefore suggest in the following an approach based on ideas coming from algebraic geometry and evaluate it against data obtained by a real power grid, located in Bavaria, Germany. After discussing the results we describe possible application scenarios.

4.1   Mathematical Background

Our modeling approach is based on the so called extended ABM algorithm (see [7]), an advancement of a group of algorithms that were developed to obtain polynomial descriptions of physical systems (see [8], [9]) The common assumption hereby is, that a certain set of measured data contains polynomial relations that describe the system under consideration. The goal is to exhibit these relations. The approach is purely data driven since only the data itself and no further assumptions are used to construct the desired models.

To make this idea precise, let $\mathbb{X} = \{p_1, \ldots, p_s\} \subset \mathbb{R}^n$ be a finite set of s measured data points, e.g., the power production of n different PV plants, measured at s points in time. The relations in question are polynomials $f \in \mathbb{R}[x_1, \ldots, x_n]$ which *vanish ϵ-approximately on* $\mathbb{X}$ for a given $\epsilon \geq 0$, i.e., $(f/||f||)(p) \approx_\epsilon 0$ for each $p \in \mathbb{X}$. Here, $|| \cdot ||$ denotes the Euclidean norm of the coefficient vector of f and $a \approx_\epsilon b$ holds for two real numbers a and b iff $|a - b| \leq \epsilon$. The threshold number ϵ thereby reflects the noise present in the data. Consider for instance the set

$$\mathbb{X} = \{(0,0), (1, 0.98), (2, 4.01), (3, 8.9), (4, 16.02)\} \subset \mathbb{R}^2 \qquad (1)$$

of 5 data points in the plane. Then the polynomial $f = y - x^2 \in \mathbb{R}[x, y]$ vanishes 0.1-approximately on $\mathbb{X}$.

To construct polynomials as desired, Limbeck [7] suggests the Approximate Buchberger-Möller (ABM) algorithm, a new combination of the Buchberger-Möller algorithm for border bases (cf. [9], [10]) and the singular value decomposition, to compute the ϵ-approximate kernel of certain evaluation matrices: Given a set of data points $p_1, \ldots, p_s \in \mathbb{R}^n$ and a threshold number $\epsilon \geq 0$, the ABM algorithm constructs a finite set $G = \{f_1, \ldots, f_t\} \subset \mathbb{R}[x_1, \ldots, x_n]$ of polynomials that vanish ϵ-approximately on $\mathbb{X}$. The Buchberger-Möller algorithm reduces the problem of finding polynomials that evaluate the given points *exactly* to zero to the problem of computing the kernel of linear mappings that come from evaluating just terms at every given point. In the approximate setting the question to compute the approximate kernel of those evaluation matrices is answered by the well organized exploitation of singular value decompositions.

The situation just described is *homogeneous* in the sense that we ask for polynomial equations with right-hand side $\approx_\epsilon 0$. If we allow a non-zero right-hand side, we accordingly ask a more general question, which we can regard as the *inhomogeneous* case. To this end, consider the *tuple* $\Xi = (p_1, \ldots, p_s)$ of s data points $p_i \in \mathbb{R}^n$ and assume that $Q = (q_1, \ldots, q_s) \in \mathbb{R}^s$ is a tuple of further data points. The goal is now to construct polynomials $f \in \mathbb{R}[x_1, \ldots, x_n]$ such that $f(p_i) \approx_\epsilon q_i$ for all $i = 1, \ldots, s$, or in other words, such that each f evaluates ϵ-approximately to Q on Ξ. An algorithmic solution to this problem is given by the *extended approximate Buchberger-Möller algorithm* (*extended ABM*, [7]). Given data points $p_1, \ldots, p_s \in \mathbb{R}^n$ combined in the tuple $\Xi = (p_1, \ldots, p_s)$, a threshold number ϵ and a tuple $Q = (q_1, \ldots, q_s) \in \mathbb{R}^s$, the algorithm constructs a finite set $G \subset \mathbb{R}[x_1, \ldots, x_n]$ of polynomials such that each $f \in G$ evaluates ϵ-approximately to Q on Ξ. To modify our example from above, we consider the tuple $\Xi = (0, 1, 2, 3, 4)$ of the points $0, \ldots, 4 \in \mathbb{R}$ together with $Q = (0, 0.98, 4.01, 8.9, 16.02) \in \mathbb{R}^5$. Then, for instance, the polynomial $f = x^2 \in \mathbb{R}[x]$ vanishes 0.1-approximately to Q on Ξ.

An important feature of all algorithms we previously mentioned, and the extended ABM in particular, is that they compute in general more than just one model polynomial. Secondly, since the extended ABM proceeds degree by degree, the constructed polynomials are of lowest degree among all ϵ-approximately vanishing polynomials. As a third feature we note, that the constructed polynomials are numerically stable with respect to perturbations in the input data set $\mathbb{X}$.

4.2   Modeling

For evaluating this mathematical approach in the context of photo-voltaic power supply, we build our investigation on real data obtained from a power grid operated by a German energy provider, Stadtwerke Passau GmbH (SWP). SWP is a local energy provider in Bavaria, Germany. More than 50% of energy generated by SWP's power plants is based on solar resources. This is why SWP seems to be a good choice for evaluating our approach. The size of the grid is 7 square kilometers large. This grid connects around 800 small scale photo-voltaic plants, which have a capacity of about 23 MWp. Most of these photo-voltaic power plants can not be measured directly: only 8 power plants are directly accessible by SWP.

Based on measurement results, we observed huge impacts of local weather effects on the amount of provided solar energy. However, no direct linear correlations between individual photo-voltaic power plants can be defined, due to the nature of photo-voltaic power generation. Since characteristics of power plants differ significantly, their relations are not expressible by linear models. These characteristics, e.g., efficiency, age, size, etc., have a high impact on the power provisioning, but there might also be other factors (e.g., local conditions) that are not obvious. Nonetheless, we assume that there might be some "hidden" non-linear correlations between power plants' generation patterns. This assumption might be realistic, since weather conditions for these plants are expected to be similar and sun irradiance does not differ significantly between their geographical locations. But instead of introducing a complex model that covers all of these parameters, we propose a methodology to derive such correlations based on mathematical analysis of power provisioning data. The analysis is purely based on power provisioning patterns obtained from photo-voltaic power plants of SWP and does not depend on any other, additional data. This means that no assumptions on weather conditions, irradiation, geographical positions and so on are being made for the evaluation. For our analysis, we use the extended ABM algorithm which detects dependencies that are approximately polynomial. If there are any correlations between power provisioning data obtained from power plants, these are detected by the algorithm.

Using the extended ABM algorithm, we aim to answer the following questions:

1. Is it, in principle, possible to model some of the photo-voltaic plants in terms of the others?

2. How many different PVs do we need to express the others?

3. How good are the approximations, especially with respect to the number of omitted PVs?

4. Can we observe local effects? Can we explain why some models are in particular good, by looking at the closeness of some PVs?

For this purpose, we observed local weather conditions and traced power supply patterns of all eight directly measured photo-voltaic power plants of SWP for three consecutive days: The first two days are characterized by a highly fluctuating solar irradiation, the third day had a continuously clear sky except early morning and evening hours, see Figure 2. To build models using the extended ABM, we proceed as follows.

1. Data selection:
   Divide the data into two sets, a training set and a validation set. In our case, we took the data of one day for training and the other two days for evaluation.

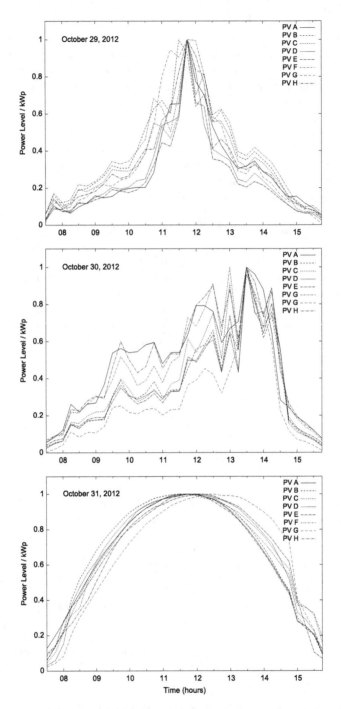

Fig. 2. Normalized measured data of eight PV power plants, taken on three consecutive days from 29 October, 2012 to 31 October, 2012

2. Target selection:
   For both the training and validation sets, divide the set of PV plants into
   two groups, a group of *source data* that will provide the input data X and
   a group of *target data* each of which serves as the right-hand side Q in the
   input of the extended ABM.

3. Preprocessing:
   Typical preprocessing steps consist, e.g., of removing invalid data, filtering
   and normalization. For the present three days, we removed the values for
   those times, where the PV plants did not produce any energy and normalized the remaining data series.

4. Model building:
   Use the training data as input for the extended ABM and obtain a set of
   polynomials G, the set of model candidates.

5. Model selection:
   Using the validation source data from the two selection steps above, evaluate
   each polynomial and compute its residual error with respect to the validation
   target. Select the polynomial with the least residual error.

4.3   Results

We applied the method described in the previous section to the data provided by
eight directly measured PV systems between 29 October, 2012 and 31 October,
2012. For further reference, we name these eight plants by the letters A to H.
The data is measured in intervals of 15 minutes. Since we considere only the
time between 7:30 and 15:45, omitting early morning and evening hours where
the stations did not produce energy, we receive for each day and each plant 34
data points, measuring the current power production.

Due to the structural similarity of the 8 data series of 31 October, which was
a clear day, we did not use that data for training but instead made two different
runs: Run 1 using the data from 29 October and Run 2 using the data from 30
October as training set. Table 3 gives an overview of Run 2. We denote by m

Table 3. Error statistics for Run 2, standard deviation in parenthesis

m	Avg. # models	Avg. best error	Avg. mean error	Best error
1	56.0 (20.8)	1.7 (3.7)	4.4 (8.0)	0.21
2	47.6 (15.0)	2.8 (6.0)	11.7 (32.3)	0.89
3	36.6 (10.6)	4.5 (10.7)	30.3 (140.4)	1.54
4	25.1 (6.2)	12.5 (59.9)	105.4 (901.0)	2.28
5	15.8 (3.3)	161.8 (1456.6)	1354.7 (13767.4)	4.77

Table 4. Target PV plants for which best residual errors were obtained

m	1	2	3	4
Run 1	C	E, F	D, E, F	C, D, E, H
Run 2	C	D, F	B, E, F	B, C, D, F

the number of PV plants that we use as target data, i.e., that we try to model in terms of the remaining $8 - m$ PV plants. There are $s_m := \binom{8}{m}$ possible ways to select those PV plants and in each run we built models for all s_m possible *selections*. Thereby, m ranged from 1 to 7, since we need at least one source data set. For $m = 6$ and $m = 7$ we did not get any reasonable model, the results are therefore omitted.

Fixing m and one of the s_m selections, we get three numbers that we use to characterize the models of the given selection: (1) the number of models returned by the AVI, (2) the least (i.e., best) residual error of these models and (3) the mean residual error of these models. Averaging those three values over all s_m selections gives the results of the second, third and fourth column of Table 3. The respective standard deviations are given in parenthesis. The last column shows the overall best error among all selections.

To make the computations comparable, we used a value of $\epsilon = 0.1$ throughout all computations. It is important to note that the value of ϵ must not be confused with the residual errors discussed above. The value of ϵ guarantees bounds within the training data while the residual error is a measure to compare validation data. It is also not surprising that the number of models decreases with increasing m. The reason is that the polynomials are constructed within $\mathbb{R}[x_{i_1}, \ldots, x_{i_{8-m}}]$ (with $i_k \in \{A, \ldots, H\}$) and therefore the number of terms per degree also decreases.

Table 4 shows the selection of target PV stations for the best model of Run 1 and Run 2, respectively. The PV stations B, C, E, F and H are all located within a radius of 1 km. Together with D they lie within a radius of 2 km. Further away are plants A and G, a radius of 3.5 km is required to surround all 8 PV plants. The results meet out expectation that close-by plants can more easily be modeled by each other.

The question how good the constructed models are depends on the demands of a concrete application and their particular requirements. We consider the models for $m = 1, \ldots, 4$ as good both with respect to the overall residual error as well as with respect to the coverage of the dynamics of the system. Figure 5 shows that the two quite distinct dynamics of 30 October and 31 October are covered equally well.

All computations were executed on a 2.26 GHz Intel Core 2 Duo laptop using the computer algebra system ApCoCoA [11]. On average, a call of the extended ABM on a 34×4 input matrix took 0.021 seconds.

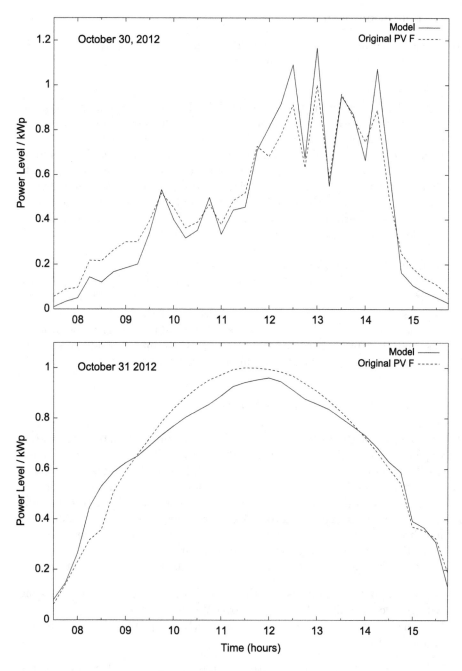

$$f_F = -1.04x_A x_B + 0.62x_C^2 + 0.40x_G^2 - 1.2x_B x_G - 1.38x_C x_H - 0.81x_G x_H + 3.31x_H^2$$
$$+ 0.37x_A + 1.43x_B + 0.81x_C - 0.06x_G - 1.52x_H + 0.02 \in \mathbb{R}[x_A, x_B, x_C, x_G, x_H]$$

Fig. 5. Best model for PV plant F in Run 1, $m = 3$ and its evaluation for the validation sets

4.4 Application Scenarios

We consider two application scenarios for the modeling approach described in the last section: Snapshot provisioning and simulation.

1. *Snapshot provisioning*
   A snapshot of the amount of power available in the grid or smaller sub-areas can help power providers or large consumers such as data centers to adapt feed or consumption parameters, thereby improving load balancing or optimizing economical goals. In this scenario, a small number of PV plants is directly measured and this data is available on-line. The data of PV plants that are not measured on-line is derived by their corresponding model polynomials. To compute these polynomials, an initial calibration phase is necessary: Over a certain period of time, data for every PV station in question is collected. From this data, the model polynomials are constructed.

2. *Simulation of power flow*
   As a straight forward variation of the first scenario, model polynomials once constructed can be used to simulate certain aspects of the grid: Varying the data used as input, one explores the behavior of the grid under different circumstances. Power flow analysis is a substantial tool for grid operators to ensure grid stability. By taking into account these interdependencies, simulation results are expected to become more accurate.

5   Conclusion and Future Work

We introduced a methodology to build models of the production of photo-voltaic power plants. In contrast to other approaches, these models also aim to be suited for small-scale areas in a small scale power grid, in addition to larger-scale scenarios. Furthermore, no external data like sun radiation or justification of the PV panels are required. The models can be used by energy providers to determine available power generated by photo-voltaic power plants (state estimation) that are not directly connected to the communication infrastructure. This *snapshot* of the grid's status can be used for monitoring purposes.

The resulting models met our expectation with respect in two directions:

- According to evaluation results, the approach seems to be quite promising with respect to geographically close-by PV plants.
- The selection of the model plants is sufficiently independent on the choice of training data.

We are confident that there is still great potential to further enhance the approach. Future work is dedicated to enhance the model by considering geographical locations of power plants. Since our evaluation results imply that modeling results for close-by PV plants lead to more precise results, this additional, domain-specific knowledge could lead to accuracy improvements. Furthermore, we think that our methodology leads to improvements in accuracy of power forecast methods. Current models do not analyze hidden interdependencies of PV plants and do not consider them for forecasting available power. This will be subject of future work.

Acknowledgments. This work has received support by the EU projects All4Green (FP7 STREP, grant no. 288674) and EINS (FP7 NoE, grant no. 288021).

References

1. Thomaschki, K.: Positionpapier zur verbesserten Prognose und Bilanzierung von Solarstromeinspeisung (2011)
2. Saint-Drenan, Y.M., Bofinger, S., Ernst, B., Landgraf, T., Rohrig, K.: Regional nowcasting of the solar power production with pv-plant measurements and sattelite images. In: Proc. ISES Solar World Congress (2011)
3. Mares, K.: Demand response and open automated demand response opportunities for data centers (2010)
4. Kennedy, B.: Power quality primer. McGraw-Hill Professional (2000)
5. Pedro, H.T.C., Coimbra, C.F.M.: Assessment of forecasting techniques for solar power production with no exogenous inputs. Solar Energy (2012)
6. Vereinigung Deutscher Elektrizitätswerke, E.V.: Umsetzung der analytischen lastprofilverfahren – step-by-step (2000)
7. Limbeck, J.: Computation of Approximate Border Bases and Applications. PhD thesis, University of Passau (to appear, 2013)
8. Held, D., Kreuzer, M., Pokutta, S., Poulisse, H.: Approximate computation of zero-dimensional polynomial ideals. Journal of Symbolic Computation 44(11), 1566–1591 (2009)
9. Kreuzer, M., Poulisse, H.: Subideal border bases. Mathematics of Computation 80(274), 1135 (2010)
10. Möller, H.M., Buchberger, B.: The construction of multivariate polynomials with preassigned zeros. In: Calmet, J. (ed.) ISSAC 1982 and EUROCAM 1982. LNCS, vol. 144, pp. 24–31. Springer, Heidelberg (1982)
11. ApCoCoA: Applied Computations in Commutative Algebra, http://www.apcocoa.org/

Energy Aware Database Management

Christian Bunse, Hagen Höpfner, Sonja Klingert,
Essam Mansour, and Suman Roychoudhury

Fachhochschule Stralsund, Bauhaus-Universität Weimar, Universität Mannheim,
King Abdullah University, Tata Consulting

Abstract. Data center and cloud providers are responsible for providing services such as storage or retrieval for large amounts of (customer
owned) data by using databsae management systems (DBMS). Service
provision implies a specific quality of service regarding performance or
security. Another factor of increasing importance is energy consumption.
Although not a top priority for most customers, the cost of energy and
thus (indirectly) the cost of service provision is key for both, customer
and provider. Typically, energy consumption is viewed as a hardware
related issue. Only recently, research has proved that software has a significant impact onto the energy consumption of a system too. Database
management systems comprise various algorithms for efficiently retrieving and managing data. Typically, algorithm efficiency or performance is
correlated with execution speed. This paper reports our results concerning the energy consumption of different implementations of sorting and
join algorithms. We demonstrate that high performance algorithms often
require more energy than slower ones. Furthermore, we show that dynamically exchanging algorithms at runtime results in a better throughput.

1   Introduction and Motivation

Database management systems (DBMS) are software systems that are in
widespread use for managing data independently of applications and underlying
hardware. Hence, application developers can utilize DBMS in order to efficiently
store and retrieve data without knowing their exact implementation (aka. black-
box view). This is especially important when it comes to hosted DBMS or cloud
services.

DBMS provide various access strategies (indexes) and retrieval algorithms
for handling and manipulating data. Typically DBMS are designed to run on
desktop computers and powerful servers. Thus, execution performance or size
(memory and harddiscs) are standard optimization factors. However, due to
rapid growth in computing power and new technologies such as cloud services,
modern DBMS stretch from desktops and servers to data centers. Services such as
Dropbox, iCloud, CloudDrive or WindowsLive moved data storage and handling
to the net. Due to the large amount of data hosted by a cloud provider, the succes
of a cloud service is related to the providers' quality of service and the efficient
usage of the resource energy. Thus, reducing energy consumption will become
an optimization factor, equal to performance an size, too.

S. Klingert et al. (Eds.): E²DC 2013, LNCS 8343, pp. 40–53, 2014.

Whereas energy optimization regarding hardware (sleep mode, speed reduction, etc.) is state of the art, only little research has been performed regarding the energy consumption of software. Especially data centers and cloud providers are using virtualization as a means for reducing energy needs. Only recently (Bunse & Höpfner 2012) it was shown that the implementation of a software system as well as the choice of algorithms and components is significantly correlated to energy consumption. In this paper we present first ideas on how to minimize the energy consumption of DBMS. Since DBMS are complex software systems, as a starting point we focus on the energy consumption of basic algorithms such as sort and join operations.

The results presented in this paper were investigated by isolated experiments using standard devices. Thus, the results can only be generalized to a certain degree and we want to point out, that more general findings need additional research with other platforms.

The remainder of the paper is structured as follows: Section 2 discusses the related work. Section 3 introduces the examined algorithms. Section 4 discusses the need for a energy related complexity metric that allows to classify and later select energy-efficient algorithms. Section 5 briefly presents the evaluation environment and discusses the underlying measurement theory. Section 6 discusses the results obtained in various empirical studies. Section 7 contains first ideas on how to adapt algorithm usage to reduce energy consumptions. Section 8 concludes the paper and gives an outlook on future research.

2   Definition and Related Work

Currently, there is no commonly accepted definition for the research field of energy aware and energy efficient software or data management. Viewed from the perspective of sustainability one can distinguish and explicitly separate to domains: (1) Green IT comprises methods and techniques for ranking, analyzing and improving the efficiency of IT-Systems by using low-power hardware, virtualization, and software optimization. (2) In contrast, Green by IT or IT2Green comprises IT solutions that help to improve energy efficiency and sustainability in other domains. Typical examples are algorithms for optimizing truck routes.

Energy efficient clearly belongs to the area of Green IT. Beneath standard benchmarks on cycle time, CPU and memory usage this explicitly addresses software induced energy consumption too. Typically, the energy consumption induced by a software artifact is directly related to usage scenarios and its interaction with its hardware and software environment.

Several research projects have been conducted regarding the topic of software related energy consumption. Published ideas fall into one of the categories (1) Hardware, or (2) Software (Jain, Molnar & Ramzan 2005). Research that belongs to the hardware category, attempts to optimize the energy consumption by investigating the hardware usage, such as (Chen & Thiele 2008, Liveris, Zhou & Banerjee 2008), and innovating new hardware devices and techniques, such as (Tuan, Kao, Rahman, Das & Trimberger 2006, Wang, French, Davoodi

& Agarwal 2006). Research in second category attempts to understand how the different methods and techniques of software affect energy consumption. Research in this category can be further classified according to the main factors affecting energy consumption: *networking, communication, application nature, memory management,* and *algorithms.* Concerning *networking* work such as (Feeney 2001, Senouci & Naimi 2005), provide new routing techniques that are aware of energy consumption. Other efforts of this category focus on providing energy-aware protocols for transmitting data (Seddik-Ghaleb, Ghamri-Doudane & Senouci 2006, Singh & Singh 2002, ?). Memory consumption is an important factor concerning a system's energy consumption. In this regard work such as (Koc, Ozturk, Kandemir, Narayanan & Ercanli 2006, Ozturk & Kandemir 2005) have provided energy-aware memory management techniques. In battery-powered systems, it is not sufficient to analyze algorithms based only on time and space complexity. Energy-aware algorithms such as (Jain et al. 2005) supporting randomness, (Potlapally, Ravi, Raghunathan & Jha 2006) focusing on cryptographic, and (Sun, Gao, Chi & Huang 2008) investigating into wireless sensor networks were published.

In *networking*, different research efforts, such as (Feeney 2001, Senouci & Naimi 2005), provide new routing techniques that are aware of the energy consumed during routing packets. Others efforts of this category focus on providing energy-aware protocols for transmitting data in wireless networks generally, such as (Seddik-Ghaleb et al. 2006, Singh & Singh 2002), and ad-hoc networks, such as (Gurun, Nagpurkar & Zhao 2006). One of the fundamental techniques proposed to reduce communication is caching technique. The efforts belonging to the *communication* category introduced several energy-aware caching techniques, such as (Shen, Kumar, Das & Wang 2005, Bardine, Foglia, Gabrielli & Prete 2007, Zhang, Chang & Zhang 2007).

Due to Java platform independence, many applications are Java-based. In *application nature*, we consider the research efforts investigating into the topic of energy consumption for the java-applications and java virtual machine, such as (Seo, Malek & Medvidovic 2007, Lafond & Lilius 2007, Badea, Nicolau & Veidenbaum 2008, Farkas, Flinn, Back, Grunwald & Anderson 2000). Memory energy is one of the major energy, which is to be saved. In *memory management*, several research efforts, such as (Koc et al. 2006, Ozturk & Kandemir 2005), have provided energy-aware memory management.

3   Sorting Algorithms

Already in the first days of computing, sorting data (numbers, names, etc.) was in the focus of research. One reason might be that although sorting appears to be "easy" its efficient execution by machines is inherently complex. Even today, sorting algorithms are still being optimized or even newly invented. When it comes to data management and information retrieval efficient sorting is a major concern concerning performance and energy consumption. In the following we describe the set of sorting algorithms that were used in the context of this study. This set was defined to comprise the major algorithms that are either used in form of library functions (e.g., quicksort), are easily programmable (e.g., bubblesort) or that are regularly taught to IT students. In other words, our goal was to cover those algorithms that are in widespread use. More details on them can be found in standard text books on algorithms and data structures such as (Lafore 2002).

Bubblesort is a simple sorting algorithm that belongs to the family of comparison sorting. It works by repeatedly stepping through the list to be sorted, comparing two items at a time and swapping them if they are in the wrong order. Bubblesort has a worst-case complexity $O(n^2)$ and in the best case $O(n)$. Its memory complexity is $O(1)$.

Heapsort is a comparison-based sorting algorithm, and is part of the selection sort family. Although somewhat slower in practice on most machines than a good implementation of quicksort, it has the advantage of a worst-case $O(n \log n)$ runtime.

Insertionsort is a naive sorting algorithm that belongs to the family of comparison sorting. In general insertion sort has a time complexity of $O(n^2)$ but is known to be efficient on data sets which are already substantially sorted. Its average complexity is $n^2/4$ and linear in the best case. Furthermore insertion sort is an In-place algorithm that requires a constant amount $O(1)$ of memory space.

Mergesort , invented by John von Neumann, is a sorting algorithm that belongs to the family of comparison-based sorting. Mergesort merge sort has an average and worst-case performance of $O(n \log n)$. Unfortunately, mergesort requires three times the memory of in-place algorithms such as insertion sort.

Quicksort is a sorting algorithm, developed by Sir Charles Antony Richard Hoare (Hoare 1962), belongs to the family of exchange sorting. On average, quicksort makes $O(n \log n)$ comparisons to sort n items, but in its worst case it requires $O(n^2)$ comparisons. Typically, quicksort is regarded as one of the most efficient algorithms and is therefore typically used for all sorting tasks. Quicksort's memory usage depends on factors such as choosing the right Pivot-Element, etc. On average, having a recursion depth of $O(\log n)$, the memory complexity of quicksort is $O(\log n)$ as well.

Selectionsort. Selection sort is a sorting algorithm that belongs to the family of in-place comparison sorting. It typically searches for the minimum value, exchanges it with the value in the first position and repeats the first two steps for the remaining list. On average selectionsort has a $O(n^2)$ complexity that makes it inefficient on large lists. Selectionsort typically outperforms bubble sort but is generally outperformed by insertion sort.

Shakersort (Brejová 2001) is a variant of shellsort that compares each adjacent pair of items in a list in turn, swapping them if necessary, and alternately passes through the list from the beginning to the end then from the end to the beginning. It stops when a pass does no swaps. Its complexity is $O(n^2)$ for arbitrary data, but approaches $O(n)$ if the list is nearly in order at the beginning.

Shellsort is a generalization of insertion sort, named after its inventor, Donald Shell. The algorithm belongs to the family of in-place sorting but is regarded to be unstable. The algorithm performs $O(n^2)$ comparisons and exchanges in the worst case, but can be improved to $O(n \log_2 n)$. This is worse than the optimal comparison sorts, which are $O(n \log n)$. Shellsort improves insertion sort by comparing elements separated by a gap of several positions. This lets an element take "bigger steps" toward its expected position. Multiple passes over the data are taken with smaller and smaller gap sizes. The last step of Shell sort is a plain insertion sort, but by then, the array of data is guaranteed to be almost sorted.

4   Energy Complexity Classification

Following (Höpfner & Bunse 2010*b*) complexity measures are one means for classifying software artifacts regarding their energy needs. In general, a complexity class is a set of problems of related resource-based complexity and is defined by the set of problems that can be solved by an abstract machine M using $O(f(n))$ of resource R, where n is the size of the input. In the context of this paper we are interested in the usage of resources. This is typically covered by the big-O notation that describes the limiting behavior of a function. It allows to simplify functions in order to concentrate on growth rates. Thus, big-O can be used to describe an algorithm's usage of computational resources (e.g., the worst case or average case running time or memory usage of an algorithm is often expressed as a function of the length of its input). This allows algorithm designers to predict the behavior of algorithms and to choose the best fitting algorithm (regarding its complexity class), in a way that is (nearly) independent of the computer architecture or clock rate. Regarding the definition of complexity class for energy we have to consider the resources involved in the computation. Therefore, we have to distinguish and explicitly separate four sub-components: $O_c(f_c(n))$ is the complexity for the CPU which is equivalent to the well known running time, since the energy consumption of a CPU is related to the number of instructions which, in turn depends on the size of the input. Similarly one can say that the complexity $O_p(f_p(n))$ corresponds to memory-usage complexity, since the energy consumption of primary memory depends on the number of read/write operations, which are derived or based on the input size. We have to point out that memory-usage complexity is *not* equivalent to the memory complexity known from theoretical computer science. The memory complexity describes the required amount of memory but does not include the memory accesses. Obviously, an algorithm could use only a constant amount of memory but read/write it several times. The same holds for the complexity $O_s(f_s(n))$ class characterizing the energy consumption of secondary memory. As the number of data transmissions is a function over the input size, too, $O_n(f_n(n))$ might express the energy complexity for the network resource. We learned from the previous chapter that energy consumptions of resources vary. Hence, we have to use the energy characteristics of the resources as scaling factors. For simplification we assume that E_c is the energy required for processing one input element, E_p and E_s for storing and retrieving one input element to/from main memory or secondary storage, respectively, and E_n for sending/receiving one input element via the network. Therefore, the energy complexity of an algorithms is given as sum:

$$O^E(f_e(n)) = O_c(E_c \cdot f_c(n)) + O_p(E_p \cdot f_p(n)) + O_s(E_s \cdot f_s(n))$$
$$+O_n(E_n \cdot f_n(n))$$

Finding the energy complexity (sub)functions As mentioned earlier, the overall energy complexity class can be notated as the sum of the class functions of the involved resource. Obviously, it is possible to analyze the program code in order to find the respective (sub)functions. However, the running time complexity for most algorithms is known. Considering only CPU and RAM usage one can find the memory-access complexity by analyzing energy measurements. We described the measurement approach used in the following in (Bunse, Höpfner, Mansour & Roychoudhury 2009). Hence, $E_c \cdot f_c(n)$ is the function of the runtime complexity multiplied with the energy required for one operation. For example, for Mergesort $f_c(n) = n \cdot \log(n)$ holds. We measured the energy for one operation E_c (in this case for one value comparison) as well as the energy $E(n)$ required by the algorithm for various n. We know, that $E(n) = E_c \cdot f_c(n) + E_p \cdot f_p(n)$ holds. Hence, we can use model fitting techniques and tools like Eureqa[1] for finding $f_p(n)$.

Example: Given the running time complexity $O(n \cdot \log(n))$ of Mergesort, the energy of $5.33 \cdot 10^{-6} J$ consumed for one comparison and the normalized overall energy $E(n)$ ($E(10) = 0.00006042J \ldots E(1000) = 0.0100312J$ consumed by executing the algorithm for various n (?), we can find the memory-access complexity $f_p(n)$ by using the target function $E(n) = 5.33 \cdot 10^{-6} \cdot (n \cdot \log(n)) + f_p(n)$. To simplify the task for the model fitter we first calculated $E(n) - 5.33 \cdot 10^{-6} \cdot (n \cdot \log(n)) = f_p(n)$, copied the data to Eureqa, and searched for $f_p(n)$. The tool found various functions, e.g. $1.02553 \cdot 10^{-5} \cdot n - 5.1406 \cdot 10^{-5} \cdot \log(0.0033665 \cdot n - 0.0236113) - 0.000269206$. Almost all of them have shown an $n - \log(n)$ structure. As we know that each comparison requires reading the comparison partners from memory, the memory access complexity of our Mergesort implementation is $O(n \cdot \log(n) + n - \log(n))$, which equals $O((n-1) \cdot \log(n) + n)$.

For analyzing the secondary storage complexity and the network complexity one could use monitoring tools for file systems and network traffic in combination with model fitting techniques.

---

[1] http://ccsl.mae.cornell.edu/eureqa

5   Measurement Environment

Based on (Höpfner & Bunse 2010a), energy requirements can be measured via examining voltage drops at sense resistors captured during the execution of a service or application. Energy can then be calculated, following Ohm's and Kirchhoff's law, by evaluating the integral of the curve defined by the data. In contrast to performance or execution time that can be measured at specific (local) points, energy is a "delocalized" property. The energy required by or for a service is the sum of the energy required by all involved components (CPU, memory, etc). Exact measures require multiple measurement points resulting in massive data sizes given that each component provides a measurement opportunity. A typical solution regarding this problem is to examine the energy demanded by a component in isolation in order to either provide a fixed value (e.g., line losses) or by defining a function (e.g., correlation to load). Energy may then be measured at a central interface. Unfortunately, it is not trivial to insert a sense resistor between, e.g., a CPU and the power supply since modern CPUs have multiple power lines. To avoid such problems we decided to use a board that offers dedicated measurement points for most components. Modern CPUs using multiple cores embedded in one chip cause another problem. A parallel execution of processes would lead to errors if energy is measured at one core only. Our first solution was to configure the system in a way that only one core is used, but we are revising our approach to address this problem.

We used a specific evaluation platform (Bunse, Klingert & Schulze 2011) In detail, the algorithms where executed on single board machine. Every program (algorithm) sent a TTL level signal (Lancaster 1974) at the start and end of its run in order to trigger measurement and logging by a digital oscilloscope. The collected data was externally processed in order to calculate the consumed energy values and stored.

6   Experimental Results

To practically evaluate the energy consumption of base energy complexity of sorting and join algorithms or queries a number of test run have been performed. All figures in this section use accumulated, non-normalized values. The following results are sums of measurement results of random, sorted and reverse-sorted data and are accumulated for 1,000 cycles.

We first examined whether software energy consumption, as widely believed, is strongly correlated to software performance. Therefore, we executed the algorithms on platforms using varying processor types. During these runs the consumed energy, execution time, and the number of cycles were recorded (data has been published in (Höpfner & Bunse 2010a)) . Results regarding the energy consumption reveal that, in contrast to the initial assumption, sorting algorithms such as Insertionsort ($O(n^2)$) require significant less energy than high performance algorithms such as Quicksort ($O(n \log n)$). I

Based on these finding a second series was started to examine the correlation between energy consumption and data size. Therefore, we concentrated on

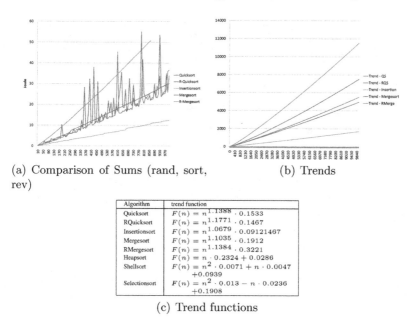

(a) Comparison of Sums (rand, sort, rev)

(b) Trends

Algorithm	trend function
Quicksort	$F(n) = n^{1.1388} \cdot 0.1533$
RQuicksort	$F(n) = n^{1.1771} \cdot 0.1467$
Insertionsort	$F(n) = n^{1.0679} \cdot 0.09121467$
Mergesort	$F(n) = n^{1.1035} \cdot 0.1912$
RMergesort	$F(n) = n^{1.1384} \cdot 0.3221$
Heapsort	$F(n) = n \cdot 0.2324 + 0.0286$
Shellsort	$F(n) = n^2 \cdot 0.0071 + n \cdot 0.0047$ $+0.0939$
Selectionsort	$F(n) = n^2 \cdot 0.013 - n \cdot 0.0236$ $+0.1908$

(c) Trend functions

Fig. 1. Experimental Results – 2nd Measurement Series

Quicksort (standard and refined), Mergesort (standard and refined), and Insertionsort with respect to random, sorted and reverse sorted data and for increasing lengths of data (0 to 1,000 elements). The obtained measurement results (Figure 1(a)) in general confirm the results of the previous experiment series by showing that Insertionsort consumes significantly less energy than other algorithms, although it is slower. In fact, sorting 1,000 randomized elements with Insertionsort took 71.3 ms, whereas Quicksort needed 8.8 ms. Regarding the second goal, we extended the platforms SRAM memory. While comparing Figure 2 and Figure 1 it becomes obvious that using external memory requires significantly more energy. For Insertionsort, e.g., the energy consumption for sorting 1,000 random elements raised from 0.03 to 4.11 Joule. The difference cannot be explained by the standard energy the additional memory requires since the differences between both curves strongly diverge with a growing data size. We assume that this is caused by moving data to/from external memory and addressing/managing these additional memory cells. The differences between algorithms become clearer by watching the interpolated trend functions in Figures 1(b) and 1(c). Here, n is the number of processed data items and the R^2 value that represents the goodness of fit was 1.

The final series investigated the energy consumption of standard join operations (see Figure 2(a)). For a small input size NLJ is most efficient, but the complexity rapidly increases as input gets bigger. By contrast, the number of HJ cycles takes grow only almost linearly, making it five times faster for input size of 300. The SMJ algorithms has two facets: for presorted data it is by far the

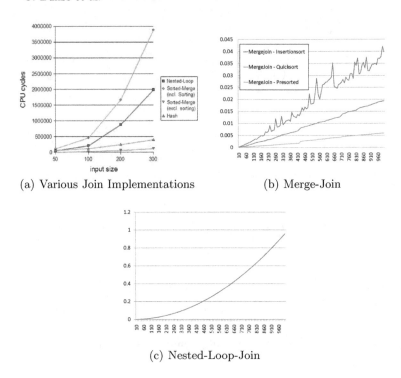

(a) Various Join Implementations   (b) Merge-Join

(c) Nested-Loop-Join

Fig. 2. Energy consumption comparison – normalized to one execution

fastest algorithm of the three, regardless of the input size. If the data has to be sorted first, the performance of the overall operation is highly slowed down by the sorting algorithm. Hence, HJ seems to be the most efficient join algorithm for unsorted input data.

From our sorting algorithm experiments we learned, that memory usage is important for energy consumptions. Whereas NLJ and SMJ (depending on the sorting algorithm used) need almost no additional memory space, HJ uses a considerable amount of memory to store the hash table. Thus, it is justifiable to assume that if considering the energy consumption instead of the performance, the outcome will be appreciably different. In order to determine the amount of energy in Joule, we measured the SMJ algorithm using Insertionsort and Quicksort. The results in Figure 2(b) conform to our previous finding that Insertionsort consumes much less energy in comparison to Quicksort. The energy consumption of a NLJ see Figure 2(c) grows quadratic. Thus, although NLJ require less execution cycles than MJ, its energy consumption is significantly higher. This supports our assumption that the energy consumption related to the execution of a specific algorithm mostly depends on its memory requirements and that the algorithms complexity class (i.e. number of execution cycles) plays a minor role.

7   Optimized Algorithm Usage

To optimize the energy consumption of modern DBMS systems via selecting energy-efficient DBMS algorithms and -queries has prerequisites. A cost model is needed that can be used to predict the cost (i.e., J or energy) for executing a specific algorithm or query on a specific input set. We developed such a model based on the energy complexity metrics introduced in section 4 and on extrapolated trend functions that calculate an estimation of the required energy for 1,000 executions [2] of an algorithm or query, based on the input size n. A selection of algorithms and queries were analyzed for defining their energy complexity measure. The reason for using both, metric and real-live data was implied by the goal of this research to find the optimal balance between performance and energy consumption.

As discussed in (Bunse, Klingert & Schulze 2012) energy consumption, performance and memory usage represent a kind of quality triangle. The cost of an algorithm or query is interrelated with other quality factors. Thus, selecting the "best" artifact cannot be based on a single criterion (i.e., energy complexity metrics or trend function). Complexity metrics characterize algorithms or queries according to their energy needs. Different algorithms/queries may be represented using the energy consumption metric. Due to the nearly linear nature of the trend function the result would always indicate Insertionsort as the most energy-efficient algorithm. In addition, both classifications neglect algorithmic complexity and performance. Therefore we applied the following strategy:

1. By using the size n of the set as an input the energy-related costs for all algorithms are calculated and stored in a table.
2. The minimum result and thus the most energy-efficient algorithm is identified.
3. Based on the algorithmic and energy complexity, the minimum value is compared to those values that are related to algorithms of "lower" complexity classes.
4. If the difference between the energy requests is below a predefined threshold or delta the "better" algorithm is chosen.

The measurements are based on the networked experimental setup (cf. Section 5). A look at the battery level V over time supports the initial assumption that the uptime of a systems is directly correlates with the energy consumption related to the executed software system. However, a closer look at Figure 3(a) shows that a non-adaptive approach (i.e., using a fixed algorithm) either results in an excellent or a poor energy efficiency. Interestingly, the results for the adaptive version are close to those of the non-optimized Insertionsort variant. Figure 3(b) supports the initial assumption concerning the trade-off between energy efficiency and performance. Fast variants like Quicksort handle more sorting requests in a shorter period of time but result in a very limited V. Energy-efficient variants like Insertionsort result in an optimal V but handle

---

[2] trend functions are build upon measurements for 1,000 execution cycles

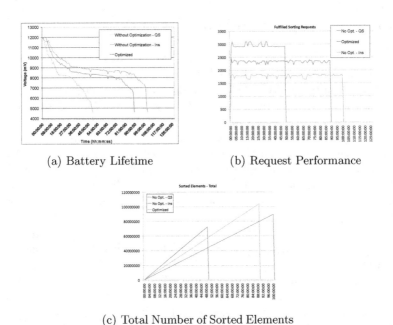

(a) Battery Lifetime   (b) Request Performance

(c) Total Number of Sorted Elements

Fig. 3. Adaptive Algorithm Selection

significantly less sorting requests. Only adaptive systems provide a good balance of energy-efficiency and performance. This is also supported by Figure 3(c) that shows the total number of elements that were sorted over time.

Recently, we started the exploration of using genetic algorithms for selecting artifacts (Wick & Phillips 2002). Genetic algorithms are a search procedure based on the principles governing natural selection in a "survival of the fittest" environment. In principle, genetic algorithms denote solutions (i.e., selections) as chromosomes, representing a specific combination of properties (i.e., performance, energy consumption, memory usage). The genetic algorithm transforms or evolves solutions to find those with an optimal fit by applying reproduction, crossover, and mutation activities. Fit is checked by performing automated test runs on dedicated machines. Results are promising and indicate that the energy needs of a DMBS system can be significantly reduced.

8   Summary, Conclusions and Outlook

We presented first results towards realizing energy aware database management for AVR micro controller based embedded systems. We concentrated on sorting and join algorithms as those are essential for query processing. We introduced our measurement setup and discussed first, preliminary results. We highlighted that memory intensive implementations consume more energy then CPU intensive ones. Interestingly, we found out that energy consumption is not solely correlated with the complexity class (performance) of an algorithm. Furthermore, we discussed first ideas on how to optimize the algorithm usage based on trend functions reflecting the energy consumption of certain algorithm implementations.

The next step on our agenda is to replicate the experiments with other platforms (i.e., PIC, ARM, and PSoC) in order to get a more generalized "cost model". Furthermore, we plan to examine other DBMS algorithms for query processing (set operations, projection, selection, etc.) and for indexing data (B-Tree, AVL trees, etc.). Afterwards, we plan to define an overall optimization strategy based on the user requirements (i.e., fast results vs. long up-time).

References

Badea, C., Nicolau, A., Veidenbaum, A.V.: Impact of JVM superoperators on energy consumption in resource-constrained embedded systems. ACM SIGPLAN Notices 43(7), 23–30 (2008)

Bardine, A., Foglia, P., Gabrielli, G., Prete, C.A.: Analysis of static and dynamic energy consumption in NUCA caches: Initial results. In: Proceedings of the 2007 Workshop on MEmory Performance: DEaling with Applications, Systems and Architecture, pp. 105–112. ACM, New York (2007)

Brejová, B.: Analyzing variants of Shellsort. Information Processing Letters 79(5), 223–227 (2001)

Bunse, C., Höpfner, H.: Ocemes: Measuring overall and component-based energy demands of mobile and embedded systems. In: Goltz, U., Magnor, M.A., Appelrath, H.-J., Matthies, H.K., Balke, W.-T., Wolf, L.C. (eds.) GI-Jahrestagung. LNI, vol. 208, pp. 434–440. GI (2012)

Bunse, C., Höpfner, H., Mansour, E., Roychoudhury, S.: Exploring the Energy Consumption of Data Sorting Algorithms in Embedded and Mobile Environments. In: ROSOC-M 2009 Proceedings (2009) (forthcoming)

Bunse, C., Klingert, S., Schulze, T.: GreenSLAs for the Energy-efficient Management of Data Centres. In: E-Energy 2011 Proc. (2011)

Bunse, C., Klingert, S., Schulze, T.: Greenslas: Supporting energy-efficiency through contracts. In: Huusko, J., de Meer, H., Klingert, S., Somov, A. (eds.) E2DC 2012. LNCS, vol. 7396, pp. 54–68. Springer, Heidelberg (2012)

Chen, J.-J., Thiele, L.: Expected system energy consumption minimization in leakage-aware DVS systems. In: ISLPED 2008: Proceeding of the Thirteenth International Symposium on Low Power Electronics and Design, pp. 315–320. ACM, New York (2008)

Farkas, K.I., Flinn, J., Back, G., Grunwald, D., Anderson, J.M.: Quantifying the energy consumption of a pocket computer and a Java virtual machine. In: SIGMETRICS 2000: Proceedings of the 2000 ACM SIGMETRICS International Conference on Measurement and Modeling of Computer Systems, pp. 252–263. ACM, New York (2000)

Feeney, L.M.: An Energy Consumption Model for Performance Analysis of Routing Protocols for Mobile Ad Hoc Networks. Mobile Networks and Applications 6(3), 239–249 (2001)

Gurun, S., Nagpurkar, P., Zhao, B.Y.: Energy consumption and conservation in mobile peer-to-peer systems. In: MobiShare 2006: Proceedings of the 1st International Workshop on Decentralized Resource Sharing in Mobile Computing and Networking, pp. 18–23. ACM, New York (2006)

Hoare, C.A.R.: Quicksort. Computer Journal 5(1), 10–15 (1962)

Höpfner, H., Bunse, C.: Energy Aware Data Management on AVR Micro Controller Based Systems. ACM SIGSOFT SEN 35(3) (2010a)

Höpfner, H., Bunse, C.: Towards an energy-consumption based complexity classification for resource substitution strategies. In: Balke, W.-T., Lofi, C. (eds.) Grundlagen von Datenbanken. CEUR Workshop Proceedings, vol. 581. CEUR-WS.org (2010b)

Jain, R., Molnar, D., Ramzan, Z.: Towards understanding algorithmic factors affecting energy consumption: Switching complexity, randomness, and preliminary experiments. In: Workshop on Discrete Algothrithms and Methods for MOBILE Computing and Communications — Proceedings of the 2005 Joint Workshop on Foundations of Mobile Computing, pp. 70–79. ACM, New York (2005)

Koc, H., Ozturk, O., Kandemir, M., Narayanan, S.H.K., Ercanli, E.: Minimizing energy consumption of banked memories using data recomputation. In: ISLPED 2006: Proceedings of the 2006 International Symposium on Low Power Electronics and Design, pp. 358–362. ACM, New York (2006)

Lafond, S., Lilius, J.: Energy consumption analysis for two embedded Java virtual machines. Journal of Systems Architecture 53(5-6), 328–337 (2007)

Lafore, R.: Data Structures and Algorithms in Java, 2nd edn. SAMS Publishing, Indianapolis (2002)

Lancaster, D.E.: TTL Cookbook. Sams (1974)

Liveris, N., Zhou, H., Banerjee, P.: A dynamic-programming algorithm for reducing the energy consumption of pipelined system-level streaming applications. In: ASP-DAC 2008: Proceedings of the 2008 Conference on Asia and South Pacific Design Automation, pp. 42–48. IEEE Computer Society Press, Los Alamitos (2008)

Ozturk, O., Kandemir, M.: Nonuniform Banking for Reducing Memory Energy Consumption. In: DATE 2005: Proceedings of the Conference on Design, Automation and Test in Europe, pp. 814–819. IEEE Computer Society, Washington, DC (2005)

Potlapally, N.R., Ravi, S., Raghunathan, A., Jha, N.K.: A Study of the Energy Consumption Characteristics of Cryptographic Algorithms and Security Protocols. IEEE Transactions on Mobile Computing 5(2), 128–143 (2006)

Seddik-Ghaleb, A., Ghamri-Doudane, Y., Senouci, S.-M.: A performance study of TCP variants in terms of energy consumption and average goodput within a static ad hoc environment. In: IWCMC 2006: Proceedings of the 2006 International Conference on Wireless Communications and Mobile Computing, pp. 503–508. ACM, New York (2006)

Senouci, S.-M., Naimi, M.: New routing for balanced energy consumption in mobile ad hoc networks. In: PE-WASUN 2005: Proceedings of the 2nd ACM International Workshop on Performance Evaluation of Wireless Ad Hoc, Sensor, and Ubiquitous Networks, pp. 238–241. ACM, New York (2005)

Seo, C., Malek, S., Medvidovic, N.: An energy consumption framework for distributed java-based systems. In: ASE 2007: Proceedings of the Twenty-Second IEEE/ACM International Conference on Automated Software Engineering, pp. 421–424. ACM, New York (2007)

Shen, H., Kumar, M., Das, S.K., Wang, Z.: Energy-efficient data caching and prefetching for mobile devices based on utility. Mobile Networks and Application 10(4), 475–486 (2005)

Singh, H., Singh, S.: Energy consumption of tcp reno, newreno, and sack in multi-hop wireless networks. ACM SIGMETRICS Performance Evaluation Review 30(1), 206–216 (2002)

Sun, B., Gao, S.-X., Chi, R., Huang, F.: Algorithms for balancing energy consumption in wireless sensor networks. In: FOWANC 2008: Proceeding of the 1st ACM International Workshop on Foundations of Wireless Ad Hoc and Sensor Networking and Computing, pp. 53–60. ACM, New York (2008)

Tuan, T., Kao, S., Rahman, A., Das, S., Trimberger, S.: A 90nm low-power FPGA for battery-powered applications. In: FPGA 2006: Proceedings of the 2006 ACM/SIGDA 14th International Symposium on Field Programmable Gate Arrays, pp. 3–11. ACM, New York (2006)

Wang, L., French, M., Davoodi, A., Agarwal, D.: FPGA dynamic power minimization through placement and routing constraints. EURASIP Journal on Embedded Systems 2006(1) (2006)

Wick, M.R., Phillips, A.T.: Comparing the template method and strategy design patterns in a genetic algorithm application. SIGCSE Bull. 34(4), 76–80 (2002)

Zhang, M., Chang, X., Zhang, G.: Reducing cache energy consumption by tag encoding in embedded processors. In: ISLPED 2007: Proceedings of the 2007 International Symposium on Low Power Electronics and Design, pp. 367–370. ACM, New York (2007)

A Data Center Control Architecture for Power Consumption Reduction

Juan Felipe Botero[1], David Rincón[1], Anna Agustí[1], Xavier Hesselbach[1],
Frederic Raspall[1], David Remondo[1],
Antoni Barba[1], Paolo Barone[2], and Giovanni Giuliani[2]

[1] Dept. of Telematics Engineering, Universitat Politècnica de Catalunya
– BarcelonaTech, Spain
{jfbotero,drincon,anna.agusti,xavierh,fredi,
remondo,telabm}@entel.upc.edu
[2] HP Italy Innovation Center, Milan, Italy
{paolo.barone,giuliani}@hp.com

Abstract. In recent years, the emergence of the cloud computing has increased the need of resources to support cloud-based services. Therefore, the role of the data centers has become essential. Following the growing of services, power consumption has increased dramatically, while the need for energy savings and CO_2 reduction has become a requirement for a sustainable world.

The All4Green project fosters collaboration between energy providers (EP), data centers (DC) and customers/end users (EU) in order to provide energy savings and CO2 emissions reduction. In this architecture, the contract binding EPs and DCs includes flexibility terms in order to allow the collaboration in the form of discounts that can be transferred also to DC customers, if they are willing to collaborate.

This paper introduces such new control architecture for the data centers oriented to energy savings. We provide a high-level view of the modules and functionalities required for achieving the collaboration goal. We describe how SLA conditions can be extended with flexible terms, how DCs can modulate their operational mode mode according to the EPs' and their own power consumption needs, and what are the new elements and functionalities that must be implemented in the DC.

Keywords: GreenSLA, Energy Efficiency, Green Data Center and Control Architecture.

1   Introduction

It has been estimated that the Information and Communications Technology industry is responsible of 2% of the global CO_2 emissions, and a similar share of global energy consumption, and the trends point towards an increase of these figures [1]. Recent research effort to save energy in ICT industry is mainly devoted to the following topics: energy-efficient hardware, energy-efficient multiprocessor and Grid Systems and

S. Klingert et al. (Eds.): E²DC 2013, LNCS 8343, pp. 54–65, 2014.

data centers, energy-efficient wireless and wired networks, and energy-efficient HVAC (heating, ventilation and air conditioning).

Data centers (DCs), due to their constant growing size, amount of information, market penetration and, especially, high-energy demand, have been a subject of research interest in the energy efficiency field. The efforts to reduce energy have been directed to servers and cooling.

Current efforts to reduce energy consumption in DCs are focused on the optimization of single IT elements [2-4] or even subsets of the IT elements that are part of a DC [5,6]. The recently finished European Union (EU) funded project Fit4Green has made notable contributions in this topic. This research project designed energy aware optimization policies for DCs where, among other solutions, it considered the federation of several DCs and showed that energy consumption could be significantly reduced by consolidating workload on fewer, more efficient servers or by intelligently re-allocating IT services to federated sites with low environmental impact.

This paper presents the control architecture in the DCs proposed by All4Green (follow-up of FIT4Green), a project funded by the European Union (EU), which is committed to devise an architecture to reduce DCs' energy consumption by 10% on top of existing strategies and the associated CO_2 emissions. One fundamental role of this control architecture is to provide the current and estimated power consumption of the IT services running in the DC, so that the DC's intelligence is able to take decisions that contribute to the energy consumption reduction.

2   Collaboration to Save Energy

All4Green considers the following **entities** in the DC ecosystem, as shown in Fig.1: Data Centers, Energy Providers (EP) that supply energy to the DCs, and End Users (EUs) or IT Customers (ITCs) that demand IT services from the DCs.

Our scenario is a composition of the aforementioned entities, which cooperate in order to improve the energy efficiency. Such cooperation is carried out by means of the communication between software **agents** acting on behalf of each entity. Agents' actions are constrained by the contractual agreements between the parties, the so-called SLA (Service Level Agreements) or SDA (Supply Demand Agreements). Such agreements are extended with energy-related flexibility and collaboration statements. The agreements describing the services to be delivered are called GreenSDA (between DC and EP) and GreenSLA (between DC and ITC) [7,8].

Energy efficiency is obtained by changing the run-time conditions (GreenSLA) of the deployed IT services. The DC Agent makes energy-aware decisions over a service due to time/calendar changes (e.g. a service may run in low performance mode during weekends) or due to a request coming from the EP (e.g. the EP asks the DC to decrease its energy consumption due to a power shortage).

The set of energy-aware decisions made by the DC Agent needs the support of an energy-aware control architecture in the DC. For these purposes a centralized control based architecture is proposed in this paper. The agents negotiate with the diverse entities to provide energy savings, while the centralized control architecture provides the functionality needed by the DC Agent to support its decision-making process.

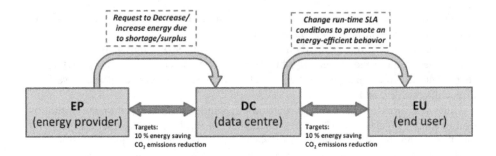

Fig. 1. Agreements, targets and actions between actors

3   The Architecture

This section describes the architecture that allows the interaction DC Agent ⇄ DC Connector ⇄ DC control system with the purpose of energy saving.

The proposed architecture is based in 3 main elements to support the required functionalities: The DC Agent, the ITC Agent and the DC Connector.

- **DC Agent**: A DC Agent represents a DC and it may interact with the DC itself, with the EP Agent that represents the EP that is supplying energy to the DC, and with the set of ITC Agents that represent the different ITCs that enjoy the services provided by the DC. Interaction with the DC is done via an element called DC Connector. This element makes it possible for the DC Agent to be agnostic with respect to the specific DC: the DC Agent will only be concerned about generic parameters that are valid for any type of DC.

- **ITC Agent:** An ITC Agent represents an ITC, and takes decisions about its own IT Services without involving any human interaction - the agent works on behalf of the ITC. It may interact with two entities associated with the DC that provides services to the ITC: the DC Agent, and the DC Connector. The ITC Agent receives queries ('collaboration requests') from the DC Agent. In such a query, the DC Agent asks whether the ITC Agent agrees in changing operating conditions of a specific active service instance. The ITC Agent responds according to the information it has on the state of the service instance.

- **DC Connector:** The DC Connector is the intermediate element between the DC Agent and the DC Control System, performing all the required functionalities from the DC Agent and the DC. The DC Connector is connected directly with the DC Control System, and it will be the driver moving actions from the DC Agent to the DC, and providing the required information from the DC to the DC Agent.

Due to its interaction either with the EP or with the ITC, the DC Agent has to take energy-aware decisions that may result in the modification of the running SLA parameters of the IT services that are deployed in the DC. The decision-making process is supported by the information coming from the interaction *DC Agent ⇄ DC Connector* about the power consumed by each service in the DC under the current conditions and also an estimation of the power that a service would consume in different running conditions. After this information has been gathered by the DC Agent, it can take an energy-efficient decision that implies the enforcement of the new running conditions for a set of IT Services in the DC.

Fig. 2 shows the interaction among the aforementioned entities. It is worth noting that the communication between the agents (DC, ITC) and the DC Connector takes place by means of three different types of messages: Generic, specific and pass-through. Each type of message triggers a different functionality in the DC Connector.

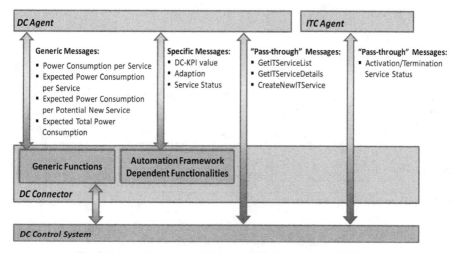

Fig. 2. Interaction among DC Agent, DC Connector and ITC Agent

3.1   General Functionality

As shown in Fig. 2, the generic functionalities of the DC Connector are triggered by the reception of any of these messages: *Power Consumption per Service* (asking for the current consumption of a running IT service), *Expected Power Consumption per Service* (asking for an estimation of the power that a specific IT service would consume over different running conditions), *Expected Power Consumption per Potential New Service* (asking for an estimation of the power that a new service would consume after deployed) and *Expected Total Power Consumption* (asking for an estimation of the total power consumed by the DC).

These functionalities are generic because they do not depend on the specifics of different data centers but they are common to all of them. The generic messages are related with power and their aim is to get current or estimated values of the power consumed either by an IT Service or by the complete DC.

To be able to provide a response to the *Power Consumption per Service* message coming from the DC Agent, the DC Connector should implement functionality that retrieves, from the DC control system, the current data necessary to calculate the current power of an IT Service. In turn, to provide a good estimation for the rest of the messages, the DC Connector rely on a Knowledge Base (KB) where historic information about the deployment and power consumption of the IT services is stored.

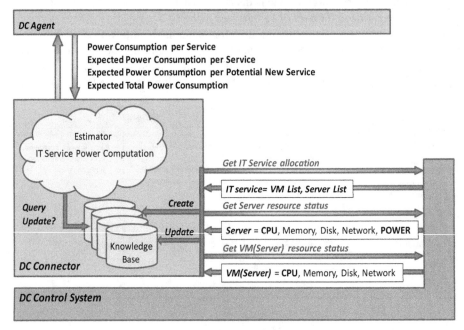

Fig. 3. DC Connector building blocks

Fig. 3 shows various components of the DC Connector that are needed to cope with the generic requests made by the DC Agent:

- *DC Connector ⇄ DC control system* **interface messages**: To calculate the amount of power used by an IT Service, the DC Connector needs to know how the service is deployed in the DC and the power consumed by the elements that host it (dedicated servers and Virtual Machines -VMs-). This information is retrieved by means of the following messages: *Get IT Service allocation* (retrieves the set of dedicated servers and VMs where the service is deployed), *Get Server resource status* (retrieves the current resource usage of the server, mainly its CPU and its power consumption) and *Get VM(Server) resource status* (retrieves the current resource usage of the VM, mainly its CPU).

- **Knowledge base**: The KB periodically polls the DC Control System to store the information of service deployment and element usage for each Time Slot (TS) making use of the aforementioned messages.

- **IT Service Power Computer**: Asking the KB for the deployment of a specific service and the current resource usage of the elements (dedicated servers, VMs) hosting it, this function calculates its current power consumption.

- **Estimator**: This functionality allows estimating the power of a running service, potential new service or completing DC, taking into account the historic register stored in the KB.

3.2   Specific Functionality

The specific functionalities of the DC Connector depend on the DC itself, i.e. they are not generic functionalities but have to be implemented taking into account the specifics of each DC. The need to implement these functionalities in the DC Connector is generated by the reception of the following messages: *Adaption/Enforcement* (asking for the enforcement of either a deployed service with different conditions or a new service) and *Service Status* (asking for the current status of a specific IT Service).

3.3   Pass-Through Functionality

This functionality of the DC Connector is very simple. Upon the reception of a pass-through request, the DC connector just passes the request to the DC control system. Also, upon the reception of a pass-through response from the DC control system, the DC Connector passes the same response to the corresponding agent.

The set of pass-through messages coming from 1) the DC Agent are: *GetITServiceList*, *GetITServiceDetails* and *CreateNewItService* and 2) from the ITC Agent are *Activation/Termination* and *ServiceStatus*.

4   Implementation Concerns

Fig. 4 shows a schema of the elements and functions that the DC Connector must implement in order to provide an answer to the generic messages sent by the DC Agent.

In the first place, either to calculate the current power consumption of a given service or to estimate the power consumption under a given combination of SLA parameters, the DC Connector must keep track of the power consumption of each Server and Virtual Machine (VM), as well as the power consumption of each IT Service during a certain time interval.

Information regarding the power consumption of Servers and Virtual Machines is obtained by periodically polling the DC using the messages defined in the interface between the DC Connector and the DC (point 1 in Fig. 4). The granularity of the polling periodicity is defined in Time Slots (TS), the duration of which is DC dependent and represents the minimum time during which the DC expects to maintain the assignment of servers and VMs almost unchanged for any IT service instance. Answers provided by the DC are stored in the Knowledge Base (point 2 in Fig. 4).

The DC Connector can directly obtain the Servers' power consumption from the DC. However, the power consumption of each VM must be inferred using some sort of algorithm to distribute the power consumption of the physical server where the VM is running on. How to design the power distribution function is also an implementation issue of the DC Connector (point 4 in Fig. 4).

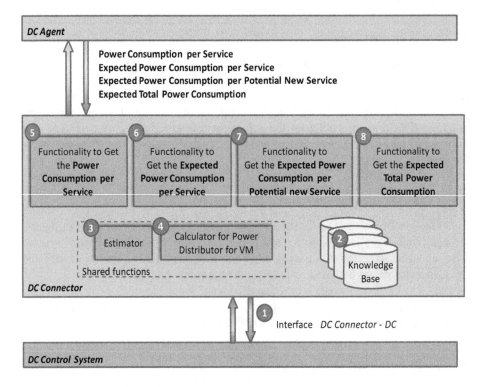

Fig. 4. Schema of the elements required to implement the generic functions in the DC Connector

The Knowledge Base (KB), in addition to the power consumption of Servers and VMs, also stores the power consumption of each IT Service. Given that the characteristics of each IT Service are described by a set of SLA parameters and given that the power consumption depends tightly on the values of such set of SLA parameters, IT Services are classified in the KB according to its type. Thus, the DC Connector requests to the DC the list of Servers and VMs assigned to a given IT Service in each TS. Then, the DC Connector calculates the power consumption of such an IT Service, and stores the result together with the list of SLA parameters and their values in the KB. Fig. 5 shows the KB's structure of tables of Servers, VMs and IT Services, as well as the messages of the interface between the DC Connector and the DC that are required to obtain the information.

The DC Connector estimates the power consumption of a given IT Service under certain operation conditions by taking a given set of values of the KB and using an estimation algorithm (point 3 in Fig. 4). The selection of which set of values are going to be retrieved from the KB as well as the specific steps to make each power computation operation depends on the implementation of the corresponding functions in the DC Connector (points 5 to 8 in Fig. 4).

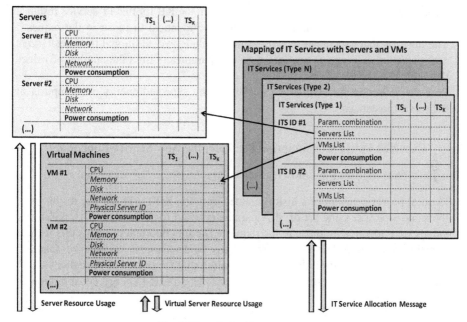

Fig. 5. Knowledge Base structure

5   Description of Functions

As shown in Fig. 4, there are four types of requests from the DC Agent to the DC Connector. To build the responses to these requests, the DC Connector will need specific functionalities, as indicated with numbers 5 to 8 in Fig. 4. Next, we describe the four different functionalities.

5.1   Power Consumption Per Service Function

This function comprises the following steps:

- The DC Connector requests the DC the resources for all servers and VMs where the service instance runs. This is done via <Get Server resources status> and <Get VM(Server) resources status> messages, respectively. Resources are for instance power consumption, CPU speed, allocated memory, and network resources.
- For each VM, calculate the Power Consumption using the power calculator.

- The Power Consumption per Service is calculated as the sum of the power consumptions of all VM and dedicated servers where the service instance runs.

5.2 Expected Power Consumption Per Service Function

This function comprises the following steps:

- Request power consumption history values from the KB for this IT service instance and for TSs when SLA parameter values were identical to those in the request[1]. The function that executes this request may include two additional parameters: *age* and *maximum number of samples*; these two parameters limit the amount of values that are passed to the caller.
- Pass the values to the estimator to establish the expected energy consumption of the service instance.

5.3 Expected Power Consumption Per Potential New Service Function

This function comprises the following steps:

- Request power consumption history values from the KB for IT service instances of the same type (i.e. same set of SLA parameters) and for TSs when SLA parameter values were identical to those in the request. The function that executes this request may include two additional parameters: *age* and *maximum number of samples*; these two parameters limit the amount of values that are passed to the caller.
- Pass the values to the estimator to establish the expected energy consumption of the service instance.

5.4 Expected Total Power Consumption Function

This function comprises the following steps:

- Request power consumption history values of all servers from the KB.
- Use the estimator to establish, for each server, its expected power consumption.
- Calculate the sum of the expected power consumptions of all servers.
- Return the sum multiplied by the Power Usage Effectiveness (PUE) factor, which incorporates the impact of cooling, UPS, etc.

6   The Power Distributor Function

To calculate the power consumed by an IT service, we need to know the power of each element (Dedicate Servers, VMs) hosting the service. The power of dedicated servers can be easily retrieved by means of the *Get Server resource status* message.

---

[1] If no data is available, the function "Expected Power Consumption per Potential New Service" will be used instead.

However, for VMs the power information is not known as it is not easy to get an idea of the exact percentage of the server's power being consumed by each of its instantiated VMs. Consequently, to define the power consumed by each VM, we make a rough estimation based on the percentage of the server CPU (in the literature the most significant element affecting power consumption [2]) that the VM is using. The calculation of this proportion is carried out using the following formula:

N = Number of servers
VM= Set of virtual machines
NC_j = Number of virtual CPUs of the virtual machine j
E_i = Energy spent by the server i, i=0,1,...,n
VL_{jk} = Load of virtual CPU k in the virtual machine j
CPU_i = CPU load of the server i, i=0,1,...,n
Per_j = Percentage of CPU load of the Virtual Machine j
VE_j = Energy spent by virtual machine j
α_{ij} = Binary value indicating whether a virtual machine j belongs to server i

$$Per_j = \left(\sum_{k=0}^{NC_j} VL_{jk}\right) \Big/ \left(\sum_{i=0}^{N} \alpha_{ij} CPU_i\right) \tag{1}$$

$$VE_j = Per_j \sum_{i=0}^{N} \alpha_{ij} E_i \tag{2}$$

The next constraint ensures that a VM can be allocated in only one server:

$$\sum_{i=0}^{N} \alpha_{ij} = 1, \forall j \in VM \tag{3}$$

7   Estimation of Energy Consumption

One key element for the aforementioned architecture to work properly and achieve the energy reduction goals is to obtain good estimations of the power consumption of each IT Service. The better the estimations, the more accurate the decisions to be made at the DC Agent (i.e. time-shifting jobs, or changing SLA levels). In our architecture, the estimator is responsibility of the DC Connector, since it is the piece that includes the Knowledge Base where past samples are stored, and it is also the module that dialogues directly with the DC.

In general, there are two approaches for the estimation: a) power-model based estimators, and b) history-based estimators. The former relies on a detailed knowledge of the servers' characteristics and other hardware involved in the delivery of the IT Service, by applying a power model (previously calibrated) that is able to compute the consumed power from the monitoring of parameters such as CPU, memory, and disk usage, and input/output activity (see [2] for an example of such a model). Given the complexity of such models, and since our design must be general enough to run on different types of servers and/or types of DCs, we decided to rely on historical records stored in the KB and the use of linear predictors and machine learning techniques.

There are two different situations that involve estimation. On the one hand, we need to know the power consumption of an already existing IT Service under certain SLA conditions. In principle, we have information about past consumptions of the same IT Service. In this case, the estimations are obtained from the energy that the IT Service consumed under the same SLA conditions; in case no such data is available, a not-so-good estimation can be obtained from the records involving the same IT Service under different SLA conditions. On the other hand, there can be a new IT Service (either coming from a federated DC or locally demanded) for which there is no past information. In this case, we rely on the categorization of services into types (e.g. web server, virtual machine) and provide an estimation based on the past consumptions of IT services of the same type.

The aforementioned procedures use an auxiliary function that ranks the "quality" of the available samples stored in the knowledge database. The quality factor is computed from an age parameter that indicates how old is the sample, the type of service, the set of desired SLA parameters expressed in the form SLA_Condition_Pair = (SLA_Condition_type: String, value: String) that is compared to the SLA conditions that held during the execution of the IT Services whose consumptions are stored, and a maximum number of past samples to be returned. The function returns the desired number of samples, ordered in terms of the quality rank.

The estimators currently in use include a) mean of the selected past samples, and b) an autoregressive model (AR) of order 1 such as

$$X_t = \varphi X_{t-1} + \epsilon_t + C \tag{4}$$

where X_t is the time series of the stored samples, ε_t is zero-mean white noise with variance equal to that of the past samples, ϕ is the normalized autocorrelation of X_t at lag 1, and C is related to the mean of the time series. Although its simplicity, and given the statistical characteristics of consumption values captured from servers in production DCs, they seem adequate for the first phase of All4Green. We are also investigating the use of machine learning techniques. In subsequent phases, the use of Principal Component Analysis (PCA) [9] will improve the accuracy of the estimation by exploiting the intrinsic correlation between the time series stored in the KB.

8   Conclusions and Future Work

This paper has presented a novel architecture to monitor and control the data centers to take intelligent decisions in order to save energy and reduce the carbon emissions.

The paper analyzes the requirements of the full ecosystem, and defines the blocks diagram and functionalities for a real test bed. The full set of SLA conditions of the services, the running modes of the data centers and history stored of the power consumed by the services are considered.

The energy savings achieved by the proposed architecture cannot be evaluated in this paper as this environment is now being implemented and tested in a set of operating DCs under the All4Green Project. The results of these tests will give leave to assess the validity of this proposal by confirming the 10% energy consumption reduction of current DCs on top of existing strategies. The results will also allow to measure the energy consumption produced by the implementation of the proposed architecture and its relationship with the overall energy saved.

An interesting branch of future research is the scalability. It is important to assure the system availability and reliability even if the number of servers to be measured increases. Such studies will be carried out during the second phase of the project, and will ensure the deployment of our approach in arbitrarily sized DCs.

Acknowledgements. This work has been partially supported by the Spanish Government, MICINN, under research grant TIN2010-20136-C03, and by the European FP7 project All4Green, grant agreement 288674.

References

1. Cisco Systems. Cisco Global Cloud Index: Forecast and Methodology, 2011-2016 (2011), http://www.cisco.com/en/US/solutions/collateral/ns341/ns525/ns537/ns705/ns1175/Cloud_Index_White_Paper.html (last accessed December 10, 2012)
2. Basmadjian, R., Ali, N., Niedermeier, F., de Meer, H., Giuliani, G.: A methodology to predict the power consumption of servers in data centres. In: Proceedings of the 2nd International Conference on Energy-Efficient Computing and Networking (e-Energy 2011), pp. 1–10. ACM, New York (2011)
3. Basmadjian, R., de Meer, H.: Evaluating and modeling power consumption of multi-core processors. In: Proceedings of the 3rd International Conference on Future Energy Systems: Where Energy, Computing and Communication Meet, e-Energy 2012, Madrid, Spain, May 9-11, pp. 12:1–12:10. ACM, New York (2012)
4. Basmadjian, R., Niedermeier, F., de Meer, H.: Modelling and analysing the power consumption of idle servers. In: 2nd IFIP Conf. on Sustainable Internet and ICT for Sustainability (SustainIT 2012), October 4-5, pp. 1–9. IEEE, Piscataway (2012)
5. Quan, D., Basmadjian, R., de Meer, H., Lent, R., Mahmoodi, T., Sannelli, D., Mezza, F., Telesca, L., Dupont, C.: Energy efficient resource allocation strategy for cloud data centres. In: Gelenbe, E., Lent, R., Sakellari, G. (eds.) Computer and Information Sciences II, pp. 133–141. Springer, London (2012)
6. Lovasz, G., Niedermeier, F., de Meer, H.: Performance tradeoffs of energy-aware virtual machine consolidation. Cluster Computing J. 15, 1–16 (2012)
7. Laszewski, G., Wang, L.: GreenIT Service Level Agreements. In: Wieder, P., Yahyapour, R., Ziegler, W. (eds.) Grids and Service-Oriented Architectures for Service Level Agreements. Springer Science+Business Media (2010)
8. Klingert, S., Schulze, T., Bunse, C.: GreenSLAs for the Energy-efficient Management of Data Centres. In: Proceedings of the 2nd International Conference on Energy-Efficient Computing and Networking, e-Energy 2011, New York, NY, USA, May 31-June 1, pp. 21–30. ACM, New York (2011)
9. Jolliffe, I.T.: Principal Component Analysis, 2nd edn. Springer Series in Statistics. Springer (2002) ISBN 978-0-387-95442-4

Modeling Data Center Building Blocks for Energy-Efficiency and Thermal Simulations

Micha vor dem Berge[1], Georges Da Costa[2], Mateusz Jarus[3], Ariel Oleksiak[3], Wojciech Piatek[3], and Eugen Volk[4]

[1] Christmann Informationstechnik + Medien
`Micha.vordemBerge@christmann.info`
[2] IRIT, University of Toulouse
`georges.da-costa@irit.fr`
[3] Poznan Supercomputing and Networking Center
`{jarus,ariel,piatek}@man.poznan.pl`
[4] High Performance Computing Center Stuttgart
`volk@hlrs.de`

Abstract. In this paper we present a concept and specification of Data Center Efficiency Building Blocks (DEBBs), which represent hardware components of a data center complemented by descriptions of their energy efficiency. Proposed building blocks contain hardware and thermodynamic models that can be applied to simulate a data center and to evaluate its energy efficiency. DEBBs are available in an open repository being built by the CoolEmAll project. In the paper we illustrate the concept by an example of DEBB defined for the RECS multi-server system including models of its power usage and thermodynamic properties. We also show how these models are affected by specific architecture of modeled hardware and differences between various classes of applications. Proposed models are verified by a comparison to measurements on a real infrastructure. Finally, we demonstrate how DEBBs are used in data center simulations.

Keywords: data centers, energy efficiency, simulations.

1 Introduction

Recent fast development of cloud computing and computational science caused growing demand for large capacities that should be delivered in a cost-effective way by distributed data centers. However, these processes led to huge amounts of consumed energy. In many current data centers the actual IT equipment uses only half of the total energy while most of the remaining part is required for cooling and air movement resulting in poor Power Usage Effectiveness (PUE) [1] values. For these reasons many efforts were undertaken to measure and study energy efficiency of data centers, for instance [2][3][4] to name a few. In order to optimize a design or configuration of data center we need a thorough study using appropriate metrics and tools evaluating how much computation or data

S. Klingert et al. (Eds.): E²DC 2013, LNCS 8343, pp. 66–82, 2014.

processing can be done within given power and energy budget and how it affects temperatures, heat transfers, and airflows within data center. Therefore, there is a need for simulation tools and models that approach the problem from a perspective of end users and take into account all the factors that are critical to understanding and improving the energy efficiency of data centers, in particular, hardware characteristics, applications, management policies, and cooling.

To cope with this problem we introduce Data Center Efficiency Building Blocks (DEBBs), which (i) provide means to to prepare descriptions and models to be easily inserted into simulations (ii) allows data center designers and analysts to take holistic view of data centers from impact of single applications up to the heat transfer and cooling process in the whole data center. Proposed building blocks contain hardware and thermodynamic models that can be applied to simulate a data center and to evaluate its energy efficiency. They are based on common formats and standards, and contain evaluation of their energy efficiency in various conditions (rather than defining maximum power only). In this way they allow, once applied in the CoolEmAll Simulation, Visualization and Decision Support Toolkit (SVD Toolkit), to integrate discrete event and Computational Fluid Dynamics (CFD) simulations [5] and enable optimization of data center energy-efficiency also for low and variable loads rather than just for peak ones as it is usually done today. The toolkit includes the repository of DEBBs, workload and application profiles, the Data Center Workload and Resource Management Simulator, CFD simulator, metrics calculator, and visualization tools. The architecture along with interactions between components and details about the SVD Toolkit can be found in [5][6].

The structure of the paper is as follows. Section 2 contains related work concerning data center building blocks and simulations of data centers. The concept of open data center efficiency building blocks is described in Section 3. In this Section we explain how we define and build profiles of data center hardware. In Section 4 we illustrate the DEBB concept by an example of DEBB defined for the Christmann RECS system along with specific models of energy efficiency and thermodynamic properties. This Section also contains a verification of models by comparison to tests on real infrastructure. Section 5 illustrates the use of DEBBs in simulations of hardware behavior for various workloads. Section 6 concludes the paper.

2   Related Work

The problem of data center energy efficiency is recently gaining more and more interest and importance so there is a lot of ongoing work both in industry and research. There are already software tools available on the market, which can be applied to simulate thermal processes in data centers. Examples of such software include simulation codes along with more than 600 models of servers from Future Facilities, SigmaDC software, CA tools, or the TileFlow application. In most cases the simulation tools are complex and expensive solutions that allow detailed modeling heat transfer in data centers. To simplify the analysis process

Romonet introduced a simulator, which concentrates on costs analysis. Instead of complex Computational Fluid Dynamics (CFD) simulations it is based on simplified computational and cost models. However it does not enable detailed heat transfer analysis. Common problem in case of commercial data center modeling tools is that they use closed limited databases of data center hardware. Although some of providers as Future Facilities [7] have impressive databases, extensions of these databases and use of models across various tools is limited. To cope with this issue Schneider have introduced the GENOME Project that aims at collecting "genes" which are used to build data centers. They contain details of data center components and are publicly available on the Schneider website. Nevertheless, the components are described by static parameters such as "nameplate" power values rather than details that enable simulating and assessing their energy efficiency in various conditions. Another initiative aiming at collection of designs of data centers is the Open Compute Project. Started by Facebook which published its data center design details, consists of multiple members describing data centers' designs. However, Open Compute Project blueprints are designed for description of good practices rather than to be applied to simulations.

In addition to industrial solutions significant research effort was performed in the area of energy efficiency modeling and optimization. For example, models of servers' power usage were presented in [8] whereas application of these models to energy-aware scheduling in [3]. Additionally, authors in [9][10] proposed methodologies of modeling and estimation of power by specific application classes. There were also attempts to use thermodynamic information in scheduling as in [11]. Nevertheless, the above works are focused on research aspects and optimization rather than providing models to simulate real data centers.

3   Open Data Center Efficiency Building Blocks

As noted, one of the main results of the CoolEmAll project is the design of diverse types of Data center Efficiency Building Blocks (DEBBs), enabling to model and simulate a data center on different granularity levels. The following subsections describe the DEBB concept, its structure, hardware- and thermodynamic models, and metrics assessing energy-efficiency.

3.1   DEBB Concept and Structure

A DEBB is an abstract description of a piece of hardware and other components, reflecting a data-center building block on different granularity levels. A DEBB contains hardware- and thermodynamic models used by SVD toolkit [5] to simulate workload, heat- and airflow, enabling (energy-efficiency) assessment and optimization of different configurations of data centers built of these building blocks (DEBBs).

Within CoolEmAll, a DEBB is organized hierarchically and can be described on following granularity levels:

1. **Node Unit** reflects the finest granularity of building blocks to be modeled within CoolEmAll - a single blade CPU module, a so-called "pizza box", or a RECS CPU module.
2. **Node Group** reflects an assembled unit of building blocks of level 1, e.g. a complete blade center or a complete RECS unit (currently consisting of 18 node-units).
3. **ComputeBox1** reflects a typical rack within an IT service center, including building blocks of level 2 (Node Groups), power supply units and integrated cooling devices.
4. **ComputeBox2** building blocks are assembled of units of level 3, e.g. reflecting a container or even complete compute rooms, filled with racks, power-units, cooling devices, etc.

Fig. 1. DEBB structure

The structure of the DEBB is shown in Figure 1. The formal specification of DEBBs along with selected formats is described in [12], and contains description of:

(a) The hierarchy of a DEBB with aggregation and position of its objects (lower level DEBBs) is described in PLMXML [13] format, allowing references to description of models or profiles in different formats, listed below.

(b) Geometrical data describing object-shapes, necessary for CFD simulation, is expressed in STL [14] format, and is referenced from the object description in PLMXML file. The combination of these two formats: PLMXML for description of the DEBB hierarchy with position of its objects (lower level DEBBs) and STL for description of object-shapes, enables to model any scene definition (needed for CFD simulation) on different granularity levels, such as a server-room consisting of cooling components, racks, power-units, and other devices. Often a geometry for CFD simulations is simplified to reduce execution time of simulations. Hence,

DEBB also contains a separate model for visualization (see point (f)). These files are optional so either STL or VRML can be used for visualization.

(c) The PLMXML file, describing DEBB hierarchy, contains for each object a corresponding reference to its technical description, DEBB Component, describing its manufacturer and model in a CIM based format. This allows a workload simulator to identify the node type being selected for workload execution and correlate it with its power-usage profile. The entire XSD schema for specification of DEBB Components is described in [12].

(d) Power-usage profile is embedded into DEBB Component and describes for each load level of a particular component type (model and manufacturer) its corresponding power-usage, enabling calculating and simulating power consumption and heat load for different utilization levels during the simulation of the workload execution. This allows assessing power-usage of workload being executed on particular component types, such as node-types.

(e) Thermodynamic profile, stating air-throughput of fans for different levels and cooling capacity of cooling devices is defined in scope of DEBB Component schema definition. Thermodynamic profile is used by workload simulator to calculate air flow - initial boundary conditions necessary for airflow and heat-distribution simulation. The entire XSD schema for specification of thermodynamic-profile is described in scope of Component Description schema, in [12].

(f) Geometrical data for visualisation of DEBB and their shapes is described in VRML format. It is referneced from PLMXML in the same manner as geometric shapes (STL format) objects for CFD simulation.

(g) Metrics are described in XML format, embedded into PLMXML with user defined values.

As mentioned, a DEBB contains models used by SVD toolkit [5] to simulate power usage and airflow caused by workloads, enabling assessment and optimization of different configurations of data centers built of building blocks. Hence, a simulation of a DEBB on level n (e.g. ComputeBox2 level), requires DEBBs of level n-1 (e.g. ComputeBox1). As the focus of CoolEmAll is to simulate thermal behavior of a DEBB to enable design of energy-efficient building blocks, it is modeled as the smallest unit in the thermodynamic modeling process. As such, the complete Node Unit is the smallest feature that will be present in a simulation. The thermodynamic processes within a Node Group are modeled using Node-Unit models, allowing to simulate accurate heat distribution within the Node-Group. The ComputeBox1 simulations will require - besides the arrangement of the Node Groups - the velocity field and temperature at the Node Group outlets over time as inbound boundary condition and will provide the room temperature over time at the outlet of the Node Group. Similarly, the simulation of compute-room (ComputeBox2) or a container will require velocity field and temperature on inlets and outlets of ComputeBox1, reducing simulation models to required level. The following sections contain descriptions of DEBB specification elements. Additionally, the general analysis and classification of metrics for evaluation of data centers and DEBBs can be found in [15].

3.2   DEBB Energy-Efficiency Profiles

Power Profile. The key characteristics of data center components is obviously their power use. However, to analyze data centers efficiency in dynamic settings power values should be known for various loads and conditions.

In the case of IT equipment the power function may depend on its power states, load or even specific applications that are executed on resources. Total power usage can be also completed by adding constant power usage of components that does not depend on load or state of resources.

Main cause of power usage and heat dissipation are processors. Generally, the power consumption of a modern CPU is given by the formula:

$$P = C \cdot V_{core}^2 \cdot f \qquad (1)$$

with C being the processor switching capacitance, V_{core} the current P-State's core voltage and f the frequency. Based on the above equation it is suggested that although the reduction of frequency causes an increase in the time of execution, the reduction of frequency also leads to the reduction of V_{core} and thus the power savings from the $P \sim V_{core}^2$ relation outweigh the increased computation time. However, experiments performed on several HPC servers shown that this dependency does not reflect theoretical shape and is often close to linear [8]. This phenomenon can be explained by impact of other component than CPU and narrow range of available voltages.

Furthermore, detailed power usage of components such as CPUs or memory are usually unavailable. For these reasons, CoolEmAll DEBBs allow users to define dependencies between power usage and resource states (such as CPU frequency) in the form of tables. If more complex dependencies must be modeled the SVD Toolkit enables definition of arbitrary functions using energy estimation plugins.

There are two basic approaches to model power usage of resources in DEBBs: static and resource load model [16].

Static model is based on a static definition of resource power usage. This model calculates the total amount of energy consumed by the computing resource system as a sum of energy, consumed by all its components (processors, disks, power adapters, etc.). More advanced versions of this approach assume definition of resource states (e.g. CPU P-states) along with corresponding power usage. This model follows changes of resource power states and sums up the amounts of energy defined for each state. In this case, specific values of power usage are defined for all discrete n states as shown in (2):

$$S_i \to P_i, i = 1, .., n \qquad (2)$$

Resource load model extends the static power state description and enhances it with real-time resource usage, most often simply the processor load. In this way it enables a dynamic estimation of power usage based on resource basic power usage and state (defined by the static resource description) as well as resource load. In this case, specific values of power usage are defined for all pairs state and load values (discretized to l values) as shown in (3):

$$(S_i, L_j) \rightarrow P_{ij}, i = 1, .., n, j = 1, ..., l \qquad (3)$$

The power usage of computing resources may strongly depend on a type of executed application [9] [10]. Therefore, CoolEmAll power profiles allows defining power usage functions for specific application classes based on application profiles. In the example of DEBB (Section 4.3) we show differences between power profiles for selected diverse applications.

Thermodynamic Profile. Thermodynamics properties include both air throughput and thermal models. While estimation of power usage $P(t)$ and air throughput $Q(t)$ in time for all nodes is sufficient to compute temperatures using Computational Fluid Dynamics (CFD) methods, we also propose thermal models that allows simplified and faster calculations. Two ways of simulations with the use of the SVD Toolkit are illustrated in Figure 2.

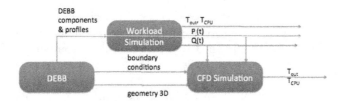

Fig. 2. Two ways of simulations with the use of the SVD Toolkit

In the first approach that assumes the use of a CFD solver to simulate detailed thermal distributions, power usage and airflow throughput must delivered as an input. Power usage is estimated based on profiles defined in Section 3.2. The airflow throughput is modeled using the air throughput profile, which enables specification of the throughput (measured in m^3/s) depending on the state of resource. The state of resource include its power state (in particular if it is on or off) but also a temperature T, which determines the air throughput level. General profile can be defined as (4). Some consideration and tests of the air throughput in a concrete server are included in Section 4.3.

$$Q = \begin{cases} 0, & \text{for node off;} \\ Q(T_0), & \text{for } T \leq T_0; \\ Q(T_i), & \text{for } T_{i-1} < T \leq T_i, i > 0. \end{cases} \qquad (4)$$

In order to create simplified thermal models of DEBBs we use basic thermodynamics rules and empirical data. For instance, for server illustrated in Figure 3 we can express dependency between power usage and change of temperature (between outlet and inlet temperature) by(5), where ρ denotes air density, Q air throughput, and C air heat capacity. However, this dependency assumes ideal case where the whole heat is dissipated into the outlet air. In practice, heat is often dissipated in other directions so to cope with this issue we introduced a parameter δ, which should be found empirically. The final formula to calculate outlet temperature is given in (6).

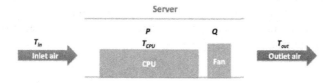

Fig. 3. Air flow in a single CPU server, section view

$$P = \rho \cdot Q \cdot C \cdot \Delta T \tag{5}$$

$$T_{out} = T_{in} + \delta \frac{P}{\rho \cdot Q \cdot C} \tag{6}$$

The example of formula derived for concrete servers and calculating δ are presented in Section 4.

4   Case Study: Building Blocks for RECS System

In this section we present a DEBB for a specific type of servers delivered by the Christmann company. Although the system provided by Christmann is a specific prototype it represents an important and emerging class of solutions that allow integrating a significant number of servers in few rack units. These solutions require more complex modeling of interrelationships between their components then traditional servers. The thermal and power usage analysis of such high-density systems is also of a great importance. For this reason, a multi-node RECS system is a good test case for illustration of DEBB design and modeling.

4.1   Efficient RECS Server Prototypes

The test case system, called RECS [5], is a high density multi-node computer that consists of 18 single server nodes within one Rack Unit. To enable the user to have a fine-grained monitoring- and controlling-system, the RECS has a dedicated master-slave system of microcontrollers integrated that can gather different metrics directly without the need of polling every single node or the need of Operation System support [2]. This enables us in the CoolEmAll project to gather many metrics like power usage, status and temperature for every node via only one request. Importantly, RECS can be equipped with diverse computing nodes ranging from high performance Intel i7 processors to Intel Atom CPUs or even embedded ARMs.

According to the DEBB hierarchy levels (defined in Section 3.1) each of RECS containing different CPUs can be defined as a separate DEBB and its model with profiles can be inserted into simulations. On the other hand, the whole set of RECS systems located in a single rack enclosure can be defined as a DEBB too. The decision depends on a scope of simulations and interests of a data center designer or analyst. In this paper we focus on modeling energy-efficiency profiles of computing nodes in a single RECS system (1 rack unit).

In the next section, we describe the actual testing environment used to construct DEBBs built on top of RECS systems.

4.2   Testbed Configuration

The testbed used to build and verify models of hardware consists of 3 RECS systems equipped with diverse kinds of CPUs. In the testbed used as a reference for building RECS models there are 3 major CPU types: Intel i7, AMD Fusion, and Intel Atom. Detailed specification of these CPUs is as follows:

- CPU: AMD G-T40N Processor @ 1GHz, CPU Cache: 512 KB, CPU Cores#: 2, RAM: 3.5 GB
- CPU: Intel Atom N2600 @ 1.60GHz, CPU Cache: 512 KB, RAM: 2 GB
- CPU: Intel Core i7-3615QE CPU @ 2.30GHz, CPU Cache: 6144 KB, RAM: 16 GB
- CPU: Intel Core i7-2715QE CPU @ 2.10GHz, CPU Cache: 6144 KB, RAM: 16 GB

Processors of each of these types are grouped in a single 18-nodes RECS system placed in one rack unit. Experiments were conducted using the Phoronix benchmark suite [17]. In particular, we run benchmarks such as pybench, c–ray, and unpack linux. In this way, we introduced various classes of applications: sequential single-core, scalable CPU-intensive, and IO-intensive computations. For each of the benchmark we imposed several load values: 25%, 50%, 75%, 100%. Additionally, we used 12.5% for Intel i7 processors to model load corresponding to a usage of one (of eights) single core (taking into account hyper-threading mechanism).

4.3   Modeling Building Blocks for RECS

Description of DEBBs for RECS is accompanied by models of servers' performance, power usage and thermodynamic properties. The models found for the configuration of the RECS system are presented in next sections. Thermodynamics properties include both air throughput and thermal models. While estimation of power usage and air throughput is sufficient to compute temperatures using Computational Fluid Dynamics (CFD) methods, we also propose thermal models that allows simplified and faster calculations as it was presented in Section 3.2.

Power Models. As presented in Section 3.2 DEBB specification allows to precisely define the power usage of modeled hardware in various states and conditions. We applied the *resource load* model, which define power usage with respect to given P-state (CPU frequency) and load. Dependencies between these values for Intel i7, AMD Fusion, and Intel Atom processors are presented in figures below.

Dependency between Load, CPU Frequency and Power Usage

Figure 4a illustrated dependency between load and power usage for selected CPU frequencies whereas Figure 4b between CPU frequency and power usage for various loads in Intel i7 CPU. While close to linear relation of power from load is usually expected, the power - CPU frequency relation does not follow theoretical quadratic (or even cubic) relation. Some possible reasons of this phenomenon are given in Section 3.2. It is also easy to see significant growth of power usage for the highest CPU frequency. Please note that for i7 processors, Turbo Boost technology is activated only for the maximum frequency. Hence power consumption and computing capabilities are different for 2300 and 2301MHz as the latter can in fact go slightly higher as long as it stays under the thermal design power (TDP).

Power profiles of RECS nodes based on AMD Fusion and Intel Atom processors are presented in Figures 4c and 4d. In case of low power Atom-based nodes power changes slightly with respect to CPU frequency and even less for changing load. In the case of AMD processors variability is also reduced mostly due to limited number of frequencies and cores. Compared to these processors Intel i7 provides large range of possible power usage and temperature values so that it makes sense to look closer to their optimal use.

Dependency between Load, CPU Frequency and Power Usage for Specific Application Classes

In CoolEmAll we model various applications including description of their phases as presented in [18]. How important is a possibility of distinction between energy efficiency of servers for various classes of applications can be seen in Figure 5. Dependency between power and CPU frequencies are presented for three different applications: single threaded pybench application, compute intensive scalable c-ray application, and IO-intensive unpacking task. As pybench application uses one core we run c-ray application with 12.5% and 25% load in order to obtain equivalent of fully loaded one logical (including hyper-threading) or physical core, respectively. The presented curves differ significantly, which shows that to obtain a precise model application classes must be taken into account. Furthermore, comparing power usage by pybench and c-ray which load the whole CPU at the same level but pybench at one core whereas c-ray evenly through all cores, we can see that the latter requires less lower power to run.

Air throughput Profile. General dependency between dissipated heat, inlet temperature and CPU/outlet temperature was briefly presented in Section 3.2. However, Christmann servers are quite specific. Flow of air from inlet to outlet through the RECS system is presented in [2] and Figure 6 (section view). This

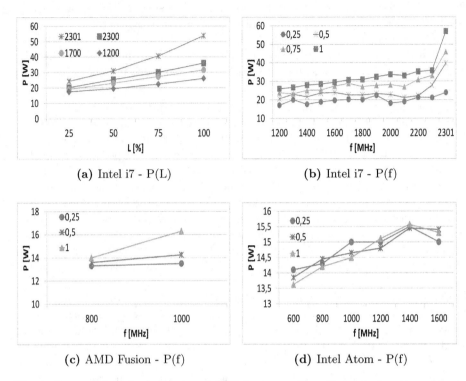

(a) Intel i7 - P(L)

(b) Intel i7 - P(f)

(c) AMD Fusion - P(f)

(d) Intel Atom - P(f)

Fig. 4. Power in function of load and CPU frequency **Top**: Power in function of load (*left*) and CPU frequency (*right*) for Intel i7 **Bottom**: Power in function of CPU frequency for AMD Fusion (*left*) and Intel Atom (*right*)

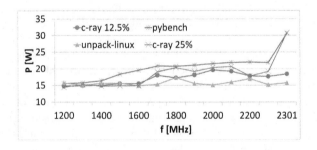

Fig. 5. Power profiles of Intel i7 processor for various applications

architecture has its consequences in the air flow properties. The mean air flow throughput of a single fan is equal to $0.22m^3/min$ (i.e. $0.0037m^3/s$) and it is constant regardless the CPU load and temperature. However, the air inside RECS enclosure can move in various directions and mix with air from other nodes. Based on our experiments the air throughput measured at the outlet and generated by the inlet node (in the first row) with the outlet node switched off was equal just to 45% of the full throughput generated by all nodes. In this way there is a dependency between power states (in this case on/off) and locations (on/off neighbors) and air throughput. This fact must be taken into account within simulation therefore should be defined within DEBB. However, for calculations of temperatures we assumed that the throughput over specific nodes inside the RECS are the same (we could not verify this assumption as we do not have air flow sensors inside enclosure of RECS).

RECS Server

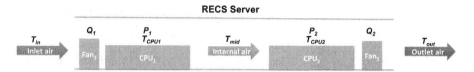

Fig. 6. Flow of air through a couple of nodes in RECS system, section view. Fans are on the side of the RECS.

Thermal Profile. The RECS architecture must be also reflected in thermal profile in DEBB. Therefore two sources of heat must be taken into account as well as two values of δ. The input temperature for CPU_2 is T_{mid} being an outlet temperature from CPU_1. Then according to (6) we define temperatures as:

$$T_{out} = T_{mid} + \delta_2 \frac{P_2}{\rho \cdot Q_2 \cdot C}, T_{mid} = T_{in} + \delta_1 \frac{P_1}{\rho \cdot Q_1 \cdot C}, \tag{7}$$

Hence, T_{out} can be calculated as follows:

$$T_{out} = T_{in} + \delta_1 \frac{P_1}{\rho \cdot Q_1 \cdot C} + \delta_2 \frac{P_2}{\rho \cdot Q_2 \cdot C}, \tag{8}$$

In order to derive values of δ_1 and δ_2, we executed tests on nodes in a single row at once (inlet row to calculate δ_1 and outlet row for δ_2) so that there was only one source of heat per each couple of nodes in one column. The obtained values were $\delta_1 = 1.78$ and $\delta_2 = 2.1$.

Having these δ values calculated and assuming the same air throughput for both inlet and outlet nodes (in case both nodes are switched on) we can model T_{out} in simulations (Section 5). However, even without simulations certain observations related to location of utilized computing nodes were made based on experiments conducted on our testbed. In Figure 8 we present 4 diverse states of a RECS system. Starting from top of the figure: (1) nodes in the second (outlet) row are loaded while nodes in the first (inlet) row are idle, (2) nodes in the first row are loaded while nodes in the second row are idle, (3) nodes in the second row are loaded while nodes in the first row are switched off, and (4) nodes in the first row are loaded while nodes in the second row are switched off. For such configurations we observed that: differences of outlet temperatures between states 1

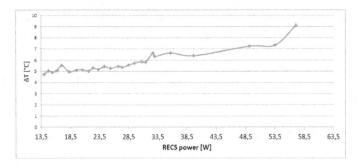

Fig. 7. Difference between outlet and inlet temperature in function of power usage

and 2 are negligible, for state 2 are much higher (2-2.5°C) than for state 4, also for state 3 are significantly higher then for state 4 (0.6-2.6°C). Interesting case is the difference between state 1 and 3. For the highest load outlet temperatures are higher in state 3 (by around 0.5°C) than in state 1 while for lower loads opposite occurs. For loads 0.75, 0.5, 0.25 and 0.125, outlet temperature in state 3 is lower than in state 1 by 0.3, 1.0, 1.1 and 1.5°C, respectively. This uncommon behavior can be explained by a support in removing hot air by a second fan of idle node in state 1. If load of the outlet node decreases gain from additional fan is reduced compared to heat dissipated by the idle node. Additionally, we noticed usual increase of temperatures for nodes under significant load close to measurement points (0.1-0.7°C). As it also happened for inlet temperatures it suggests that this change is caused by heat dissipated in other ways than passed by flowing air.

5   Application of Models in Data Center Simulations

DEBBs available in the CoolEmAll repository can be used in tools being part of the SVD Toolkit [5] to simulate and analyze energy-efficiency of data centers. One of these tools is a Data Center Workload and Resource Management Simulator (DCworms) [16][19]. In general, DCworms allows modeling and simulation of data center computing infrastructures to study their performance and energy-efficiency. As explained in Section 3.2, it can be used as a tool providing input (power usage, air throughput) to heat transfer CFD simulations or as a simulator that provides rough estimations of temperatures, too. To this end, we use DCworms to verify power usage and thermodynamic models proposed in previous sections and perform experiments in order to get insights into a few examples of management policies.

5.1   Verification of Models

In the first step simple experiments reflecting tests in real environment were performed to verified obtained models. These models include two issues: (i) modeling

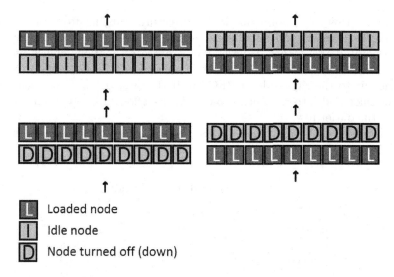

L   Loaded node
I   Idle node
D   Node turned off (down)

Fig. 8. Various configurations of switched on/off and loaded/idle computing nodes in RECS system (States: 1, 2, 3, 4 starting from the top)

and estimating power usage and (ii) modeling and estimating outlet temperatures. Results of this verification are briefly summarized below.

The application of power profiles in a simulation environment allows estimating power usage of hardware components based on load and P-state of the system. While we were able to include all measured values of P-states the load had to be discretized (to 25%, 50%, 75%, and 100%). To estimate power usage for load in between values defined in the profile we used linear interpolation. The mean error of such estimation exceeded slightly 2W, from 0.62W to 4.22W for various frequencies and load ranges. Overwhelming majority of errors were overestimations. Factors that especially affected the accuracy of prediction included hyper-threading mechanism and Turbo Boost mode in the Intel i7 processor, which are difficult to model.

Proposed outlet temperature estimation models along with calculated δ values gave mean errors 0.78 and 0.81 degree Celsius, respectively. For both inlet and outlet nodes switched on at the same time errors were slightly bigger so for more detailed heat transfer analysis CFD simulations are needed taking as an input the power usage and air throughput delivered by DCworms. Generally, CoolEmAll users have these two options to choose depending on purpose and timeline of their experiments.

5.2   Simulation Experiments

Using DCworms we simulated execution of workloads on resources defined by DEBBs for RECS. In particular, to increase the accuracy of obtained results, we performed our experiments for one single homogeneous RECS unit based on i7 nodes. However, more complex architectures ranging from racks up to the whole data center can also be evaluated. For the experimental purposes, we incorporated the proposed outlet temperature estimation models into the DCworms. Jobs were managed by 3 simple policies: *left2right* - allocating jobs from the left to the right side of RECS in both rows, *in2out* - allocating jobs from the inlet nodes to the outlet row, *out2in* - allocating jobs from the inlet nodes to the outlet row.

The details of a workload used in this experiment are presented in Table 1.

Table 1. Workload characteristics

Characteristic	Load intensity		Distribution
	30	70	
Task Count		1000	constant
Task Interval [s]	1200	560	poisson
Load		0.0 - 1.0	uniform
Application class	Scalable CPU-intensive		uniform - 33%
	Single threaded		uniform - 33%
	IO-intensive		uniform - 33%

The Table 2 summarizes the results. As expected, that greater load results in higher outlet temperatures. Moreover, even if mean outlet temperatures are similar between different policies, the variability of these temperatures may differ. Additionally, for policies *out2in* and *in2out* differences between standard deviation are opposite for various workloads (in this case 30 and 70%).

Table 2. Mean outlet temp (°C) and standard deviation for 30% and 70% workload

policy	30%			70%		
	left2right30	in2out30	out2in30	left2right70	in2out70	out2in70
mean	26.96	26.87	27.15	28.79	28.72	28.89
std. dev.	1.99	0.715	0.83	1.68	1.00	0.85

This simple example of DCworms usage demonstrates how DEBBs can be applied within SVD Toolkit to study energy-efficiency of data centers, in particular to topics such as capacity management, power capping, and thermal-aware scheduling. Additionally, to study phenomena such as air turbulences and heat transfers within the whole data center, the Computational Fluid Dynamics (CFD) simulations are applied. To this end, we use CoolEmAll SVD Toolkit tools that take as an input DEBB geometry models and boundary conditions from the output of workload simulations presented in this section.

6   Conclusions

In this paper, we presented a concept of open Data Center Efficiency Building Blocks (DEBBs) - descriptions and models of hardware that can be used to build and enhance data centers. The role of DEBBs is to provide models that can be easily inserted into simulations (both of workloads and heat transfer) and visualization. Hence, a DEBB consists of several parts defined in common or standard formats where possible. We demonstrated the DEBB concept on an example of a prototype multi-node high-density system called RECS. We presented power usage and thermodynamics models, which can be applied to more complex simulations of data centers. To perform these simulations larger number of DEBBs along with models of additional devices such as UPS must be added. To analyze air flow processes in more detail CFD simulations should be applied which, although out of the scope of this paper, are part of the CoolEmAll SVD Toolkit functionality. DEBBs defined within CoolAmAll project are available through the DEBB repository at the CoolEmAll website [20]. Among future work we plan to improve precision of thermodynamic models and add more energy-efficiency and performance information for well defined application classes. We are going to apply prepared DEBBs in various simulation studies including tests with management policies as well as data center cooling infrastructures.

Acknowledgements. The results presented in this paper are partially funded by the European Commission under contract 288701 through the project CoolEmAll and by a grant from Polish National Science Center under award number 636/N-COST/09/2010/0.

References

1. The Green Grid Data Center Power Efficiency Metrics: PUE and DCiE, http://www.thegreengrid.org/Global/Content/white-papers/ The-Green-Grid-Data-Center-Power-Efficiency-Metrics-PUE-and-DCiE
2. Kipp, A., Schubert, L., Liu, J., Jiang, T., Christmann, W., vor dem Berge, M.: Energy Consumption Optimisation in HPC Service Centres. In: Topping, B.H.V., Ivanyi, P. (eds.) Proceedings of the Second International Conference on Parallel, Distributed, Grid and Cloud Computing for Engineering. Civil-Comp Press, Stirlingshire (2011)
3. Mammela, O., Majanen, M., Basmadjian, R., De Meer, H., Giesler, A., Homberg, W.: Energy-aware job scheduler for high-performance computing. Computer Science - Research and Development 27(4), 265–275 (2012)
4. The MontBlanc project website, http://www.montblanc-project.eu/
5. vor dem Berge, M., Da Costa, G., Kopecki, A., Oleksiak, A., Pierson, J.-M., Piontek, T., Volk, E., Wesner, S.: Modeling and Simulation of Data Center Energy-Efficiency in CoolEmAll. In: Huusko, J., de Meer, H., Klingert, S., Somov, A. (eds.) E2DC 2012. LNCS, vol. 7396, pp. 25–36. Springer, Heidelberg (2012)
6. Woessner, U., Volk, E., Gallizo, G., vor dem Berge, M., Da Costa, G., Domagalski, P., Piatek, W., Pierson, J.-M.: D2.2 Design of the CoolEmAll simulation and visualisation environment - CoolEmAll Deliverable (2012), http://coolemall.eu

7. Future Facilities, `http://www.futurefacilities.com/`

8. Basmadjian, R., Ali, N., Niedermeier, F., de Meer, H., Giuliani, G.: A methodology to predict the power consumption of servers in data centers. In: Proceedings of the 2nd International Conference on Energy-Efficient Computing and Networking 2011 (e-Energy). ACM, New York (2011)

9. Da Costa, G., Helmut, H., Karin, H., Jean-Marc, P.: Modeling the Energy Consumption of Distributed Applications. In: Handbook of Energy-Aware and Green Computing. Chapman & Hall, CRC Press (2012)

10. Witkowski, M., Oleksiak, A., Piontek, T., Weglarz, J.: Practical power consumption estimation for real life HPC applications. Future Generation Computer Systems 29, 208–217 (2012)

11. Mukherjee, T., Banerjee, A., Varsamopoulos, G., Gupta, S.K.S.: Model-driven coordinated management of data centers. Comput. Netw. 54(1), 2869–2886 (2010), `http://dx.doi.org/10.1016/j.comnet.2010.08.011`, doi:10.1016/j.comnet.2010.08.011

12. Hoyer, M., vor dem Berge, M., Volk, E., Gallizo, G., Buchholz, J., Fornos, R., Siso, L., Piatek, W.: D3.2 First definition of the modular compute box with integrated cooling - CoolEmAll (2012), `http://coolemall.eu`

13. PLM XML Schema, Siemens (January 8, 2013), `http://www.plm.automation.siemens.com/legacy/products/open/plmxml/docs/v6.0.2/PLMXMLSchema.xsd`

14. The STL Format (January 8, 2013), `http://www.ennex.com/~fabbers/StL.asp`

15. Sis, L., Forns, R.B., Napolitano, A., Salom, J., Da Costa, G., Volk, E., Donoghue, A.: D5.1 White paper on Energy- and Heat-aware metrics for computing modules - CoolEmAll Deliverable (2012), `http://coolemall.eu`

16. Kurowski, K., Oleksiak, A., Piatek, W., Piontek, T., Przybyszewski, A., Weglarz, J.: DCWoRMS - a tool for simulation of energy efficiency in distributed computing infrastructures. Simulation Modelling Practice and Theory (to appear, 2013)

17. `http://www.phoronix-test-suite.com/`

18. Chetsa, G.L.T., Lefevre, L., Pierson, J.-M., Stolf, P., Da Costa, G.: DNA-Inspired Scheme for Building the Energy Profile of HPC Systems. In: Huusko, J., de Meer, H., Klingert, S., Somov, A. (eds.) E2DC 2012. LNCS, vol. 7396, pp. 141–152. Springer, Heidelberg (2012)

19. Bak, S., Krystek, M., Kurowski, K., Oleksiak, A., Piatek, W., Weglarz, J.: GSSIM - a Tool for Distributed Computing Experiments. Scientific Programming 19(4), 231–251 (2011)

20. CoolEmAll DEBB Repository, DEBB Repository, `http://coolemall.eu`

A Simulator to Assess Energy-Saving Techniques in Content Distribution Networks

Tom Bostoen[1], Jeff Napper[1], Sape Mullender[1], and Yolande Berbers[2]

[1] Alcatel-Lucent Bell Labs,
Copernicuslaan 50, B-2018 Antwerpen, Belgium
{Tom.Bostoen,Jeff.Napper,Sape.Mullender}@alcatel-lucent.com
http://www.alcatel-lucent.com/bell-labs
[2] Katholieke Universiteit Leuven,
Celestijnenlaan 200A, B-3001 Heverlee, Belgium
Yolande.Berbers@cs.kuleuven.be
https://distrinet.cs.kuleuven.be

Abstract. The scalable and bandwidth-efficient delivery of IPTV services to an increasingly diverse set of screens requires the deployment of *telco* content distribution networks (CDNs). These CDNs are composed of cache servers located in the telco's data centers close to the end user. The additional cache servers need to be designed for energy efficiency to limit the increase of data-center energy consumption. We analyze real HTTP adaptive-streaming traces from an operational telco CDN delivering IPTV to mobile devices to identify workload characteristics that can be exploited to conserve energy. We also present a trace-driven simulator that models the energy consumption of such a CDN down to the level of the cache-server disk to evaluate potential energy-saving techniques. The traces reveal cyclic load fluctuations that can be exploited to save energy in CDNs by varying the number of powered cache servers and disks according to the load.

Keywords: Content distribution network, HTTP adaptive streaming, cache server, energy efficiency, disk drive, power reduction.

1 Introduction

Because consumers want to watch videos on every screen they own, Internet service providers are starting to extend their IPTV offering with online multi-screen video services. ISPs can deliver video streams from content providers to their clients by means of their own content distribution network (CDN) for a superior viewing experience. Such *telco* CDNs [1], which are composed of disk-packed cache servers deployed in the ISP-owned regional network close to the end users, ensure a scalable, bandwidth-efficient delivery of both linear and on-demand video streams. Data centers consume globally 1 to 2 % of all available power and their power consumption grows by 15 % a year [2]. The deployment of additional power-hungry cache servers in data centers to build new telco CDNs can be expected to accelerate the increase in data-center power consumption.

S. Klingert et al. (Eds.): E²DC 2013, LNCS 8343, pp. 83–98, 2014.

In this paper, we target energy savings in content distribution networks by approaching the CDN as a storage system distributed over multiple data centers, thereby exploiting the state-of-the-art in power-aware storage systems. We present the following three research contributions. As our main contribution, we propose a trace-driven CDN energy-consumption simulator based on the common linear model for the energy consumption of a cache server as a function of the server load [3] and the known model for the energy consumption of a disk drive as a function of disk read and write accesses [4]. The simulator includes a model for traditional hard disk drives as well as solid-state disks. It allows transitioning a cache server from the idle mode to the standby mode and the other way around. Such transitions can also be applied to individual disks of a cache server. The simulator allows trading off energy consumed by the caches (and their disks) against CDN scalability (or throughput) and bandwidth efficiency. For this initial release of the simulator, we don't model the location of the caches in the network. Consequently, the load balancing over the caches doesn't take the proximity between client and cache into account. We intend to support geographical load balancing in the next iteration of the simulator. We plan to release the simulator as free and open-source software to accelerate the research in this domain through collaboration.

As a supporting second contribution, we provide a first-cut characterization of the multiscreen (tablet and smartphone) IPTV workload used to drive the simulator. We present the most relevant workload characteristics of the HTTP adaptive streaming traces collected from an operational telco CDN delivering exclusively IPTV services. The file download bandwidth as a function of time exhibits a diurnal pattern of large load fluctuations to a great extent consistent with observations for similar workloads, e.g. IPTV delivered to the traditional TV screen only [5] and user-generated video-on-demand [6].

The simulator is based on known models. Therefore, we don't present a validation of the simulator. Instead, we present interesting simulation results based on the IPTV workload traces at the level of the disk, cache server, and CDN as derived third contribution. Simulation reveals that CDNs are far from *energy-proportional* [3]. This lack of energy proportionality leads to energy waste because of the fluctuations in the workload. This waste can be reduced by applying a power-reduction technique known for data-center storage systems as DIV [7] (short for diverted accesses) to content distribution networks.

The remainder of the paper has the following outline. Section 2 describes the workload characterization. In Section 3, we present the CDN simulator. Simulation results are described in Section 4. In Section 5, we describe related work. Finally, Section 6 is the conclusion of our paper.

2   Workload Characterization

In this section, we search for CDN workload characteristics that can be exploited to save energy in the CDN. We start from workload traces produced by an operational telco CDN delivering IPTV (live broadcast TV and video-on-demand) to mobile screens (smartphone and tablet) by means of HTTP adaptive streaming. The combination of the widespread use of wireless terminals, even in the home, and the large bandwidth variation exhibited by wireless connections drives the adoption of HTTP adaptive streaming as the protocol for delivering on-line video services [8]. For HTTP adaptive streaming, the source video stream is encoded at different bit rates. These different-bit-rate streams are partitioned in short, constant-duration segments. The segment files are stored in the origin server together with index files, which provide an ordered list of references to segment files. For live television, the index files provide a frequently regenerated rolling snapshot of the broadcast. Using HTTP, the client fetches segments one after the other (according to the index) from a cache, which might then fetch it from the origin. The client selects every segment such that the segment's bit-rate encoding is adapted to the network conditions.

The traces contain information about all HTTP responses delivered by any of the CDN caches during one calendar day. We analyze the seven consecutive traces of a week during the Fall of 2012. We subsampled the traces by randomly selecting clients. The resulting subsampled traces contain the information of about ~1.4 billion HTTP responses and have a total zipped-file size of ~48 GiB. Our analysis results in (1) the probability mass function (pmf) of the downloaded file and (2) the file download bandwidth as a function of time. Figure 1 shows the estimated pmf of the downloaded file. We consider all files (solid line), the index files only (dashed line), and the segment files only (dash-dot line). The pmf estimation involves counting the number of downloads per unique file during one week. This table of download frequencies is divided by the total number of unique files. This division leads to relative frequencies. The files are ranked according to their download frequency. The roughly ~3000 files that are downloaded most frequently appear to be downloaded at a significantly higher rate than the rest of the files. These turn out to be the index files that are continuously fetched for live streams. Even when we only consider segment files, the pmf doesn't appear to be linear in the log-log scale.

Figure 2 shows the file download bandwidth as a function of time. This download bandwidth is calculated by adding up the sizes of the HTTP responses per 60-s time interval (during which the HTTP response was sent) and dividing by 60 s. The figure reveals a cyclic load fluctuation that can be explained based on end user behavior. During the day, most people are working and therefore the load on the caches is low. In the evening more people start watching videos until ~21:30 when the load on the caches peaks. After this peak, the load drops as people presumably go to sleep. In the morning (~7:30) before people generally go to work, there is a smaller load peak. During the weekend, the load fluctuation is naturally somewhat different from the fluctuation on a weekday. In addition to the daily and weekly load variation, there might also be seasonal load fluctuations as well as a gradual load variation caused by the changing number of subscribers to the service. A large load variation over long time intervals can be exploited to save energy by activating at any point in time only the number

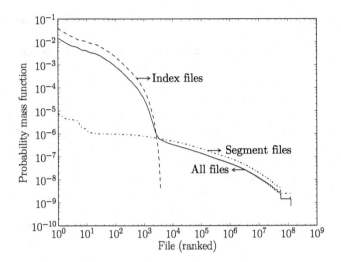

Fig. 1. Probability mass function of the (ranked) downloaded file for all files, the index files only, and the segment files only

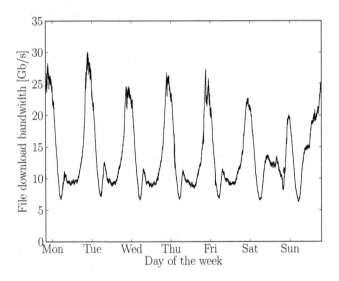

Fig. 2. File download bandwidth (from caches to clients) over a single week

of caches and disks required to support the load at that moment, as will be explained in Section 4.

To the best of our knowledge, we are not aware of any work characterizing exactly the type of workload we consider in this paper: IPTV (live and on-demand) delivered to mobile devices (smartphones and tablets) by means of HTTP adaptive streaming over a telco CDN. Nevertheless, it does make sense to compare our results with the characteristics of slightly different workload types such as traditional IPTV, i.e., live TV delivered to TV screens, on the one hand [5] and user-generate videos streamed on-demand on the other hand [6]. We are especially interested in comparing the load fluctuations. A traditional IPTV workload shows cyclic load fluctuations similar to the ones shown in Figure 2 although we observe a slightly more pronounced peak in the morning and the large peak at ~15:00 observed in [5] is missing in Figure 2. Also a web-based video-sharing workload [6] shows daily load variations but the traffic peaks in the afternoon (between ~14:00 and ~18:00), thus earlier than IPTV.

3   CDN Energy Simulator

In this section, we describe a trace-driven CDN energy-consumption simulator, which can be used to evaluate potential techniques for saving energy in content distribution networks. Our Python-based simulator uses the workload traces described in Section 2 as input. The CDN model used as basis for our simulator is described next.

3.1   CDN Model

In practice, when a client wants to access one of the video streams on the origin, a combination of DNS indirection and HTTP redirection redirects the client to the best cache server. Commonly used request-routing policies would select the cache server that is closest to the client and not overloaded. However, our traces do not group clients geographically, and the initial release of our simulator described in this paper does not consider location. Therefore, we selected a request-routing policy for the simulator that balances the load across the cache servers without consideration of distance between client and cache. A new client to the CDN is redirected to the active cache server with the lowest load. The simulator allows turning off caches to save energy. Every succeeding HTTP request from a client gets redirected to the same cache server. Only when that cache is overloaded or powered-down does the simulated request-routing system redirect the client to another cache server, again with the lowest load.

   The simulator models *cooperative pull-based* content outsourcing where cache servers don't prefetch files from the origin: a file is pulled from the origin upon a cache miss. A cache may be considered a surrogate server or reverse proxy because it distributes content on behalf of the origin. Caches located in the same rack could cooperate; for example, using the Internet Cache Protocol (ICP). When a cache doesn't have a requested file in memory or disk, it could first try to fetch this file efficiently from one of its neighboring caches in the same rack before going to the origin. Although the simulator supports cooperative content outsourcing, we assume for simplicity that there is only one cache server per rack.

   The simulated cache server applies *multi-level* caching wherein the server fetches the requested file from, in order of priority, its memory, one of its disks, one of its neighboring caches (in the same rack), or the origin. Initially in pull-based caching, a file requested by a client is not available in the cache server. The server first fetches the file from the origin (or possibly from its neighbors), then delivers it to the client, and finally caches it in its primary memory. New files are always cached in memory. When memory is full, least-recently-used (LRU) files are moved to a disk to make space available for caching a new file. The least-loaded disk is selected to balance the load across all disks. When a disk is full while a new file needs to be stored on it, least-recently-used files are removed until the new file fits in the freed space. Thus, the simulator applies the common LRU cache replacement policy both for memory and disks.

The simulator models the CDN's energy consumption attributed to its cache servers. The energy consumption of the disks (§ 3.2) in the caches is modeled separately from the servers (§ 3.3). The simulator includes an energy-consumption model for both traditional hard disk drives as well as solid-state disks. The consumed energy is logged per time interval $T_{res} = 60\,\mathrm{s}$ (by default) for the duration of the workload trace. The total energy consumed by the CDN corresponds to the total amount of energy consumed by the cache servers the CDN is composed of, and the total energy consumed by a cache server is the sum of the energy consumed by the server excluding disks and the energy consumed by each of the server's disks. We only consider energy consumed directly by the cache servers; we ignore the additional energy required for hosting these servers in a data center (such as energy for cooling and network access). The goal of energy-saving techniques for content distribution networks is to reduce the CDN's energy consumption without unacceptable performance degradation.

3.2   Disk Energy-Consumption Model

The power consumed by a hard disk drive (HDD) depends on its activity. When a disk is idle, it consumes P_{id}^{dsk}. When seeking, the disk consumes P_{sk}^{dsk}. When reading or writing, the disk is in the active power state and consumes P_{act}^{dsk}. Finally, the disk can be spun down to the standby power state in which it consumes P_{sb}^{dsk}. The current simulator ignores the energy required to spin a disk down or up.

When the disk receives a request i to read or write a file at time t_i, it takes (1) time T^{sk} (on average) to move the actuator arm to the required cylinder, (2) time T^{rt} (on average) to wait until the right sector has rotated under the read/write head, and (3) time T_i^{tf} to transfer the file. For sake of simplicity, we assume that every file is contiguously laid out on disk. We ignore the underestimation of the seek energy that may occur as a consequence of this assumption. The transfer time (milliseconds) is a function of the file size S_i^{file} (KiB) and the transfer rate R_{tf} (MiB/s): $T_i^{tf} = 1000 S_i^{file}/(1024 R_{tf})$. The total time $T_{req,i}^{dsk}$ spent by a disk to handle request i is the sum of the seek time, rotational latency, and transfer time for that request, i.e., $T_{req,i}^{dsk} = T^{sk} + T^{rt} + T_i^{tf}$. The total time T_j^{dsk} a disk is busy addressing all requests received during time interval j is given by $T_j^{dsk} = \sum_{jT_{res} \le t_i < (j+1)T_{res}} T_{req,i}^{dsk}$. The simulator enforces the constraint

$T_j^{dsk} \leq T_{res}$ to avoid overloading a disk. Any request that does not fit within this constraint is addressed by the cache server by fetching the requested file directly from the origin. The total energy $E_{req,i}^{dsk}$ consumed by a disk to handle request i is given by $E_{req,i}^{dsk} = P_{sk}^{dsk}T^{sk} + P_{id}^{dsk}T^{rt} + P_{act}^{dsk}T_i^{tf}$. The total energy E_j^{dsk} an active disk consumes during a time interval j may be expressed as $E_j^{dsk} = (T_{res} - T_j^{dsk})P_{id}^{dsk} + \sum_{jT_{res} \leq t_i < (j+1)T_{res}} E_{req,i}^{dsk}$. A disk in the standby mode during time interval j consumes the amount of energy $E_j^{dsk} = P_{sb}^{dsk}T_{res}$.

Although traditional hard disk drives are usually preferred when capacity matters most, solid-state disks (SSDs) can be much faster for high I/O workloads. We model the energy consumption of solid state disks similarly as hard disk drives but with the following differences. The transfer rate for reading is different from the rate for writing. In addition, also the active read power is different from the active write power. Finally, we note that an SSD doesn't require seeking, or incur rotational latency. Our simulator supports solid-state disks and provides numeric values for all model parameters for two SSD types: HP 120GB 3G SATA SFF MDL SSD and HP 200GB 3G SATA MLC SFF [9]. These SSD types are used in cache servers deployed in operational CDNs. For the HP 120GB disk, the idle power is 0.1 W, the read power 1.5 W, the write power 1.9 W, the transfer rate for reading 230 MiB/s, and the transfer rate for writing 180 MiB/s. For the HP 200GB disk, the idle power is 1.3 W, the read power 1.8 W, the write power 3.4 W, the transfer rate for reading 257 MiB/s, and the transfer rate for writing 235 MiB/s. We assume that 80 % of the disk capacity can be used for caching files. We assume that the SSD standby power is 0 W.

3.3   Cache Server Energy-Consumption Model

The power consumed by a cache server depends on the server's load. This load is determined by the server's download rate $R^{srv,dn}$, where we define downstream as the direction towards the clients. This download rate varies over time and therefore depends on the time interval j, i.e., $R_j^{srv,dn}$. The simulator calculates $R_j^{srv,dn}$ as follows: Every HTTP response i with size S_i^{resp} (in bytes) is sent by the server towards the client at time t_i during a certain time interval j (where $jT_{res} \leq t_i < (j+1)T_{res}$) and therefore adds a rate $r_i^{srv,dn} = 8S_i^{resp}/(10^9 T_{res})$ (in Gb/s) to the server's download rate $R_j^{srv,dn}$ (in Gb/s), i.e., $R_j^{srv,dn} = \sum_{jT_{res} \leq t_i < (j+1)T_{res}} r_i^{srv,dn}$. The request-routing system enforces the constraint $R_j^{srv,dn} \leq R_{max}^{srv,dn}$ to avoid overloading a cache server (with maximum download rate $R_{max}^{srv,dn}$). When a client request cannot be handled by a cache server because of this constraint, the client is redirected to another cache server (the one with the lowest load). If all cache servers are overloaded, the request is dropped.

The load λ_j on the cache server during time interval j is defined by $\lambda_j = R_j^{srv,dn}/R_{max}^{srv,dn}$. This implies: $0 \leq \lambda_j \leq 1$. The power consumed by a fully-loaded ($\lambda = 1$) cache server is given by P_{max}^{srv}. However, this power includes the power consumed by the cache disks for which we use a separate disk-specific energy-consumption model (§ 3.2). We can derive the power P_{max}^{srv-} consumed by a fully-loaded cache server excluding disks by subtracting from P_{max}^{srv} the power consumed by the cache disks, i.e., $P_{max}^{srv-} \approx P_{max}^{srv} - N_{dsk}P_{act}^{dsk}$. The power consumed by the disks of a fully-loaded cache server is approximately the power consumed by all N_{dsk} disks in the active mode P_{act}^{dsk} where we assume that all disks are of the same type. For an SSD, we assume 80 % read activity and 20 % of write activity, i.e., $P_{act}^{dsk} = 0.8P_r^{dsk} + 0.2P_w^{dsk}$.

The power consumed by an idle ($\lambda = 0$) cache server is given by P_{id}^{srv}. This power includes the power of the idle cache disks. We derive the power P_{id}^{srv-} consumed by an idle cache server excluding disks as expressed by $P_{id}^{srv-} = P_{id}^{srv} - N_{dsk}P_{id}^{dsk}$. The power P_j^{srv-} of a cache server excluding disks with load λ_j at time interval j is modeled as a linear function of this load, i.e., $P_j^{srv-}(\lambda_j) = P_{id}^{srv-} + \lambda_j(P_{max}^{srv-} - P_{id}^{srv-})$. The simulator allows transitioning cache servers to a standby mode in which the server consumes P_{sb}^{srv-}. Similar as for the disks, the current simulator ignores the energy required for such transition. The energy consumed by a cache server excluding disks is given by $E_j^{srv-} = P_j^{srv-}T_{res}$. Combining the results of this section and the previous one, the energy consumed by a cache server including disks is $E_j^{srv} = E_j^{srv-} + \sum_{k=0,1,...,N_{dsk}} E_{j,k}^{dsk}$.

The simulator implements this cache-server energy-consumption model and provides numeric values for all model parameters for an HP Proliant server as an example. Such a server is equipped with a Dual Intel Xeon 5600 processor, 144 GiB of DDR3 RAM, 2 300 GiB SAS disks, and 14 120 GiB SSD disks. This cache server contains $N_{dsk} = 14$ cache disks of type HP 120GB specified in Section 3.2. However, we can simulate the energy consumption of such a server with any number of cache disks of any type as explained previously in this section. The server's idle energy excluding disks is 224.6 W. The server's maximum download rate is 18 Gb/s. At this rate, the server excluding disks consumes the maximum power 405.88 W. We assume the cache-server standby power to be 0 W. In addition, we assume that 80 % of the memory can be used for caching files.

4   Simulation Results

In this section, we demonstrate the capabilities of the CDN simulator and based on the simulation results, we identify DIV as a power-reduction technique applicable to content distribution networks. We present the results of a simulation of a CDN composed of two cache servers filled to capacity with disks. The cache servers are located in different racks so there is no inter-cache traffic. We drive the simulation by means of a one-day subsampled trace (as previously described) recorded on a Sunday by an operational CDN.

The simulated CDN is different from the operational CDN. For the simulation, we use the minimum number of cache servers required to serve all requests in the trace at any time interval, and we provision the maximum number of cache disks in the cache servers so as to maximize the cache hit ratio. Both cache servers in our simulation are HP Proliant servers, which are introduced in Section 3.3. The simulated servers each contain 14 solid-state cache disks of type HP 200GB as specified in Section 3.2. Since we currently don't consider location, adding more cache servers doesn't improve performance. On the contrary, if we add a cache server, the clients get distributed over more cache servers due to load balancing. This distribution leads to diminished file sharing among clients and therefore a smaller cache hit ratio. Moreover, limiting the number of cache servers to the minimum required for serving all requests also leads to a conservative estimate of the energy savings. At the start of the simulation the caches are empty. The cache memory fills up in ~10 min; the cache disks are full after ~10 h. In the following sections, we present the simulation results for (1) one of the disks, (2) one of the cache servers, and (3) the complete CDN. Note that the results are very similar for all disks and all cache servers because of the load balancing.

4.1 Disks

Per time interval, the disk's energy consumption depends on the disk reads and writes during the interval. Therefore, we first present Figure 3, which shows the disk read and write throughput as a function of time. The disks are not heavily loaded because the load is distributed over all 14 disks. The maximum observed write throughput represents roughly ~10 % of the maximum write throughput supported by the disk (235 MiB/s), while the maximum observed read throughput corresponds to approximately only ~1 % of the maximum read throughput that the disk can handle (257 MiB/s). Such a write-dominated workload is abnormal for cache disks and reveals an opportunity for improving the design of the simulated CDN. Provided the memory-based cache is large enough, there is no benefit to writing video segments of live streams to disk. Eliminating these unnecessary disk writes would save energy and improve the disk cache hit rate.

Because the load on the disk is small, the power consumed by the disk only exceeds the idle power at most by roughly 10 % as shown in Figure 4. For this HP 200GB SSD the idle power is 1.3 W, the active read power is 1.8 W, and the active write power is 3.4 W. The load on the disk varies over time by a factor of ~2, whereas the power consumed by the disk only varies by roughly 10 %. This discrepancy exposes the disk's lack of energy proportionality.

4.2 Cache Servers

The energy consumed by a cache server depends on its load. The download rate determines the cache load. Figure 5 shows the download rate over a single day and divides this rate in memory cache hits, disk cache hits, and cache misses. Every cache miss requires a file upload from the origin server. The maximum download rate for this type of HP Proliant server is 18 Gb/s. The cache hit ratio (including memory and disk cache) is approximately 80 % and remains more or less constant during the entire day. There are relatively few disk cache hits because (1) the linear video streams can be served directly from primary memory because it is large enough and (2) on-demand video represents only about 5 % of the data requested by clients.

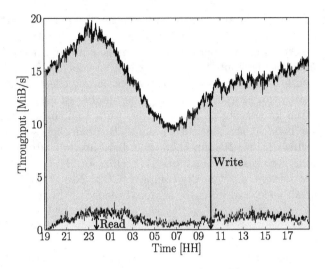

Fig. 3. Single cache-server disk read and write throughput over a single day

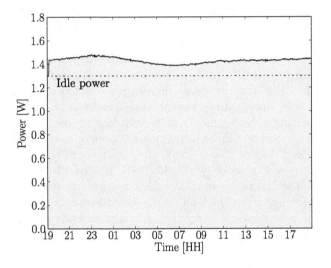

Fig. 4. Single cache-server disk power consumption

The load fluctuation over the day causes a similarly fluctuating power consumption as shown in Figure 6. This figure also divides the consumed power between the cache disks and the cache server excluding disks. The maximum power consumption of this type of cache server (including 14 HP 200GB disks) is approximately 435.56 W, whereas the idle power consumption is 242.8 W. For the type of cache server and disks under consideration, the power consumed by the disks represents about 5 % of the total power consumed. This ratio strongly depends on the disk type and is significantly higher for hard disk drives for which

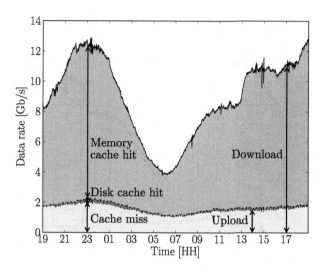

Fig. 5. Single cache-server data rate over a single day divided in memory cache hits, disk cache hits, and cache misses

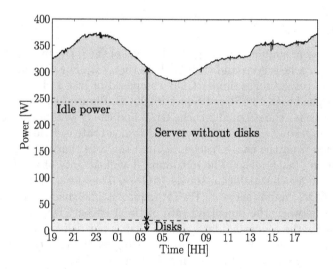

Fig. 6. Single cache-server power consumption over a single day divided between disks and server

we don't present simulation results in this paper to save space. Like a disk, a cache server is far from energy proportional as a comparison of Figure 6 and Figure 5 reveals.

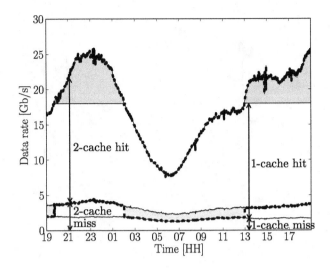

Fig. 7. Download and upload rate (cache miss) for a 1-cache CDN (thin solid), 2-cache CDN (thin solid), and DIV-enabled 2-cache CDN (thick dashed) over a single day

4.3   CDN

Finally, we present simulation results at the level of the CDN by aggregating the results of the 2 cache servers and their 28 disks (in total). For comparison, we add the simulation results for a similar CDN composed of just 1 HP Proliant cache server also packed with 14 SSDs of type HP 200GB. Figure 7 shows the download and upload rate for the original 2-cache CDN and the newly-introduced 1-cache CDN over a single day. For both CDNs, the download rate is divided into the rate served directly from the cache (cache hit) and the rate that requires uploading from the origin (cache miss). The maximum download rate of the HP Proliant cache server under consideration equals 18 Gb/s. Therefore, during prime time the 1-cache CDN cannot serve all HTTP requests. The shaded area at the top of the figure between the download rate of the 1-cache CDN and the 2-cache CDN represents the requested data volume that is not delivered by the 1-cache CDN. For the 2-cache CDN, the upload rate is higher than for the 1-cache CDN because a 2-cache CDN exhibits less file sharing than a 1-cache CDN.

Figure 7 shows the power consumed by the 2-cache and 1-cache CDN. Obviously, the 1-cache CDN consumes less power than the CDN composed of 2 cache servers. The total energy consumed over the day under consideration by the 2-cache CDN amounts to 15.25 kWh, whereas the 1-cache CDN consumes only 9.67 kWh. Thus, both from an energy as well as a performance perspective, the 1-cache CDN outperforms the 2-cache CDN during the time periods where the requested download rate does not exceed the maximum rate a single cache server can deliver.

Comparing Figure 7 and 8 reveals that the CDN is far from energy proportional. For example, while the data rate delivered by the CDN decreases from

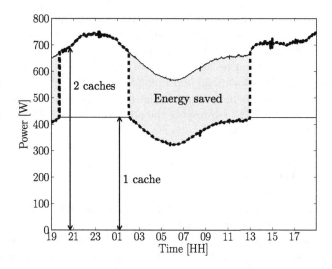

Fig. 8. Power consumed by a 1-cache CDN (thin solid), 2-cache CDN (thin solid), and DIV-enabled 2-cache CDN (thick dashed) over a single day

~25 Gb/s to ~7.5 Gb/s, i.e., by ~70 %, the power consumed by the CDN decreases by only ~25 %. This energy disproportionality is caused by the significant idle power consumed by both cache servers and disks. The CDN is provisioned to cope with the peak load and therefore overprovisioned under moderate to light load. Energy can be saved by the application of *dynamic power management* (DPM), which reduces power consumption by turning off system components or decreasing their performance when they are idle or underutilized [10]. In datacenter storage systems, DPM may be enabled by diverting disk accesses from redundant to original disks using a technique called DIV [7]. Similarly we propose to turn off cache servers and disks under moderate to light load. Cache servers and their disks can be powered-down relatively easily because they only contain replicated data, but performance constraints in a real CDN would also need to be considered. When a cache server is powered down, clients can be directed to one of the caches that remain active. When a disk is turned off and the requested file is stored on that disk, the cache server can fetch the file either from one of its neighbors (in the same rack) or from the origin. Devices may be powered down completely or alternatively transitioned to a standby mode. In the future, we intend to adapt DIV to content distribution networks and evaluate this energy-saving technique using our CDN energy simulator.

Figure 8 illustrates DIV-based energy savings. Suppose we turn off one of the caches of the 2-cache CDN whenever the requested download rate is smaller than 18 Gb/s, then we would save 2.84 kWh or, equivalently, 20 %, which the shaded areas of Figure 8 represent. The thick dashed line corresponds to the power consumed by the DIV-enabled 2-cache CDN. Even though we provisioned just the minimum number of caches required to handle the workload, the energy savings are significant. Taking a realistic overprovisioning into account (to cope with larger fluctuations caused by, for example, flash crowds), would yield even more energy savings. Additionally, scalability is maintained and bandwidth efficiency even improved as can be observed from Figure 7. The thick dashed lines in Figure 7 represent the download and upload rate of the DIV-enabled 2-cache CDN. The shaded area on the bottom of the figure between the upload rate of the 1-cache and 2-cache CDN represents the additional data volume that can be served directly from the cache.

5 Related Work

Over the last ten years many power-reduction techniques for data-center storage systems were proposed. We present an exhaustive survey of such energy-saving techniques in [4] based on an analysis of over a hundred high-quality papers. To our knowledge, the state-of-the-art in power-aware storage systems does not yet include content distribution networks although such networks are composed of storage elements distributed over multiple data centers. In this paper, we propose to adapt a power-reduction technique called DIV [7] (short for diverted accesses) to content distribution networks as explained in Section 4. The inherent segregation of original and redundant data in a CDN facilitates the application of DIV to CDNs. Instead of diverting accesses from redundant disks, accesses in a CDN are diverted from underutilized cache servers.

Even though power-reduction techniques for storage systems have not yet been applied to content distribution networks, recently the energy efficiency of CDNs in general has become an area of active research. The focus of this research is on energy-aware cache-server placement and file replica placement. [11] compares the energy consumed by delivering content (1) directly from storage servers centralized in a data center, (2) from cache servers of a CDN, and (3) from neighboring clients using P2P delivery. The CDN architecture turns out to be the most energy efficient. Similar results were obtained by [12] in the context of IPTV delivery. [13] claims even higher energy savings by placing the caches in the home gateways. Content-centric networking (CCN) integrates cache servers into routers and therefore eliminates the need for an overlay content distribution network. [14] claims that CCN is even more energy-efficient than a traditional CDN. [15] refines this claim by revealing the dependency on content popularity and catalog size. In this paper, we consider only the CDN architecture and don't take the location of the cache servers into account. Therefore, we don't model the transport energy but only the energy required by the cache servers. However, this server energy is modeled in much greater detail. We use this detailed cache-server energy consumption model as the basis for a trace-driven CDN energy simulator to evaluate energy-saving techniques based on dynamic power management.

Recently, research results were presented about energy-aware load balancing in content distribution networks [2], which is similar to the energy-saving technique of diverted accesses. However, Mathew et al. focus on the energy-aware load-balancing algorithms, whereas our focus is on a trace-driven CDN energy simulator that allows evaluating potentially different energy-saving techniques. To the best of our knowledge, no CDN energy simulators exist; only CDN performance simulators are available [16].

6 Conclusion

The massive end-user demand for IPTV on any screen spurs the deployment of telco CDNs for HTTP-based adaptive video streaming. The disk-packed cache servers of which such CDNs are composed add to the energy consumption of data centers, which is a growing concern to data-center operators. In this paper, we target energy savings in these content distribution networks. Therefore, we analyze the HTTP-adaptive-streaming workload from an operational CDN delivering IPTV. This workload exhibits cyclic fluctuations, which can be exploited to save energy. In addition, we present a CDN energy simulator, which can be used to evaluate energy-saving techniques in content distribution networks. Simulation results reveal that typical CDNs are far from energy proportional. Therefore, we propose to apply a power-reduction technique for storage systems called DIV to content distribution networks. The adapted technique would turn off complete cache servers or individual cache disks under moderate or light load. In the future, we plan to propose algorithms for determining the minimum number of cache servers and disks that need to stay on to satisfy performance requirements. In addition, we want to make the current simulator location-aware such that we can observe latency and transport energy trade-offs and support geographical load balancing.

Acknowledgments. The authors would like to thank their colleagues of Velocix, an Alcatel-Lucent company, and Koen Laevens for their support in getting access to CDN workload traces. In addition, this work is supported by the Flanders Agency for Innovation by Science and Technology (IWT), grant IWT 100690.

References

1. Alcatel-Lucent: Velocix (2012), http://www.velocix.com
2. Mathew, V., Sitaraman, R., Shenoy, P.: Energy-aware load balancing in content delivery networks. In: Proceedings of the 31st Annual IEEE International Conference on Computer Communications, INFOCOM 2012, pp. 954–962. IEEE, Los Alamitos (2012)
3. Barroso, L.A., Hölzle, U.: The case for energy-proportional computing. Computer 40, 33–37 (2007)
4. Bostoen, T., Mullender, S., Berbers, Y.: Power-reduction techniques for data-center storage systems. ACM Comput. Surv. 45(3), 33:1–33:38 (2013)
5. Cha, M., Rodriguez, P., Crowcroft, J., Moon, S., Amatriain, X.: Watching television over an ip network. In: Proceedings of the 8th ACM SIGCOMM Conference on Internet Measurement, IMC 2008, pp. 71–84. ACM, New York (2008)

6. Gill, P., Arlitt, M., Li, Z., Mahanti, A.: Youtube traffic characterization: a view from the edge. In: Proceedings of the 7th ACM SIGCOMM Conference on Internet Measurement, IMC 2007, pp. 15–28. ACM, New York (2007)

7. Pinheiro, E., Bianchini, R., Dubnicki, C.: Exploiting redundancy to conserve energy in storage systems. SIGMETRICS Perform. Eval. Rev. 34, 15–26 (2006)

8. Begen, A., Akgul, T., Baugher, M.: Watching video over the web: Part 1: Streaming protocols. IEEE Internet Computing 15(2), 54–63 (2011)

9. HP: Hp solid state drive (ssd) for proliant server (2011),
   `http://h18000.www1.hp.com/products/quickspecs/13415_div/13415_div.pdf`

10. de Micheli, G., Benini, L.: System-level power optimization: Techniques and tools. ACM Trans. Des. Autom. Electron. Syst. 5, 115–192 (2000)

11. Feldmann, A., Gladisch, A., Kind, M., Lange, C., Smaragdakis, G., Westphal, F.J.: Energy trade-offs among content delivery architectures. In: Proceedings of the 9th Conference on Telecommunications, Media and Internet Techno-Economics, CTTE 2010, pp. 1–6. IEEE, Los Alamitos (2010)

12. Baliga, J., Ayre, R., Hinton, K., Tucker, R.: Architectures for energy-efficient iptv networks. In: Proceeding of the 2009 Conference on Optical Fiber Communication, OFC 2009, Washington, DC, USA, OSA, pp. 1–3 (2009)

13. Valancius, V., Laoutaris, N., Massoulié, L., Diot, C., Rodriguez, P.: Greening the internet with nano data centers. In: Proceedings of the 5th International Conference on Emerging Networking Experiments and Technologies, CoNEXT 2009, pp. 37–48. ACM, New York (2009)

14. Lee, U., Rimac, I., Kilper, D., Hilt, V.: Toward energy-efficient content dissemination. IEEE Network 25(2), 14–19 (2011)

15. Guan, K., Atkinson, G., Kilper, D., Gulsen, E.: On the energy efficiency of content delivery architectures. In: Proceedings of the 4th International Workshop on Green Communications, GreenComm4, pp. 1–6. IEEE, Los Alamitos (2011)

16. Stamos, K., Pallis, G., Vakali, A., Katsaros, D., Sidiropoulos, A., Manolopoulos, Y.: Cdnsim: A simulation tool for content distribution networks. ACM Trans. Model. Comput. Simul. 20(2), 10:1–10:40 (2010)

Data Center Smart Grid Integration Considering Renewable Energies and Waste Heat Usage

Stefan Janacek[1], Gunnar Schomaker[1], and Wolfgang Nebel[2]

[1] R&D Division Energy, OFFIS, Oldenburg, Germany
{janacek,schomaker}@offis.de
[2] Department for Computer Science, C.v.O. University of Oldenburg, Oldenburg, Germany
nebel@informatik.uni-oldenburg.de

Abstract. Data center (DC) power consumption is a topic of interest and research activities. Articles handle power saving by using virtualization technologies and server consolidation. We assume these technologies as base, but we want DC to profit from local renewable energy sources, reducing CO2 emissions. We propose the idea of integrating DC into smart grid, respecting location dependencies. We present our concept consisting of two individual simulations, a smart grid and a DC simulation, which are both combined to create a holistic simulation. Special focus is placed on a new DC model, the Surrogate DC Model (SDCM), and its functionality and requirements. The SDCM acts as DC, but it can adapt itself and its architecture to different energy scenarios. Goal is to obtain the best possible synergy effects between DC and smart grid in terms of energy exchange and infrastructure usage. Concepts introduced in this paper are work-in-progress.

Keywords: Data Center Effiency, Green IT, Smart Grids, Energy Management, Waste Heat Usage, Modelling, Simulation.

1 Introduction

The power demand of components of the Internet and Communication Technology (ICT) is rising since the last few years [1]. The growing demand for cloud computing and of mobile services usage [2] plays a significant role for this trend. This has lead to a significantly higher demand of power for data centers, pushing up their operational costs. The European Commission states that today, data centers consume about 2% of the entire power demand, this value is expected to double soon [3].

To reduce these costs and to comply with environmental requirements, several power saving methodologies for data centers have emerged, including server consolidation using virtualization technologies [4]. Current virtual machine migration strategies create a virtual machine distribution for optimal server usage with the aim of power savings [5,6,7,8]. Unused servers can be powered off, all active servers should be used up to their maximum capacity. These approaches

S. Klingert et al. (Eds.): E²DC 2013, LNCS 8343, pp. 99–109, 2014.

enable a data center to regulate its server load and thus the power consumption of power related components.

Meanwhile, the idea of integrating data centers into power networks such as smart grids has emerged, where the specific power consumption of a data center will become a challenge. Smart grids include several power generators and consumers, partly heavily dynamic, for example due to the usage of renewable energy sources. These are mostly intermittent energy sources (solar radiation, wind) and power is produced for example by photovoltaics or wind energy converters. A data center could act as a power balancer in such a grid, cutting power peaks or decreasing computational reserves in times of power shortages.

The usage of waste heat, the data center's servers and other components generate, is another reasonable use case in a smart grid. Here, schools, theaters, malls and other public and private facilities are potential consumers. Because of conduction losses and minimum heat energy requirements, the data center needs to generate thermal energy with specific constraints to make this scenario profitable[1]. Here again, the data center's utilization distribution may become a regulator for the power consumption and thus for the outcoming heat. There are already several existing data centers that exemplify that this concept is well working [9] and a promising approach.

Finally, a data center can profit from the infrastructure of the smart grid. Modern smart grids may contain long-term energy storages like Pumped-Storage Hydroelectricity (PSH) and Compressed Air Energy Storage (CAES) or short-term storages like e-car batteries [10] or fly wheels.

Here, we present the idea of a data center integration into an existing smart grid scenario as described above. By using simulation systems for both worlds, the data center and the smart grid world, and combining these, we want to find an optimal strategy of integrating a specific data center into an existing smart grid location or to find the optimal data center architecture for a certain location. The optimization aims to improve not only the data center's energy efficiency, but the efficiency of the smart grid including the data center as a whole. It also aims at operating the data center almost exclusively with renewable energies. Therefore, a metric to measure the success of the project should rather be the Carbon Usage Effectiveness (CUE) [11] than the Power Usage Effectiveness (PUE) [12]. The resulting simulation could help data center operators to optimize their existing data center or data center planers to find a well suited data center architecture for a new facility.

The paper is organized as follows: In Sect. 2, we provide some preconditions needed to understand our simulation concept, which is explained in Sect. 3. Section 4 introduces the Surrogate DC Model, one of the key aspects of our simulation concept. In 5, we list the related work, followed by our future research in 6 and the conclusion in Sect. 7.

---

[1] See   http://www.energyefficiencyasia.org/docs/ee_modules/Chapter-Waste
%20Heat%20Recovery.pdf

2   Preliminaries

There has already been some research in the area of optimizing the energy efficiency of data centers. However, in this area, it is important to define the meaning of the term *data center*, since a (modern large-scale) data center hosts numerous different subsections and crafts. In our research, we want to optimize the energy efficiency of the entire data center, including components for infrastructure, cooling, power management and IT. Therefore, when we use the term *data center* in this paper, the facility including all of its components just mentioned is meant.

We do not provide a concept for virtualization optimization in this paper, however we use certain strategies as a base for our work.

The idea presented in this paper bases on the fact that a data center's power consumption, especially of the servers, can be regulated by adjusting the load of individual servers [13]. This load may either be controlled by the amount and quality of incoming tasks or by applying a virtualization and migration strategy that tries to consolidate unused servers. In our concept we assume that the data center is fully virtualized, meaning that all or almost all applications run on virtual machines and that these can be live-migrated among all servers. In this context, throughout the paper, we will refer to the term *virtual machine* meaning an application and its operating system, both running inside one virtual machine. As stated in [13], this technology lets the data center operate in a power range, defined by a minimal power consumption DC_{Pmin} that is needed to power all components without any load, and a maximum consumption DC_{Pmax} that occurs in times of full load. So, for the power consumption at each time $DC_P(t)$ the following equation counts:

$$DC_{Pmin} \leq DC_P(t) \leq DC_{Pmax} \tag{1}$$

This power range is the result of control mechanisms that affect the data center's load and task distribution, but without affecting its architecture.

3   Simulation Concept

Our simulation concept consists of two simulation areas, which are combined to achieve an overall simulation. These are the smart grid simulation and attached to it a simulation system of a complete data center. In our current research, we focus on the development of the models for the data center components and their architecture, not on the smart grid simulation itself. Here, we use an existing smart grid simulation framework that is currently developed at OFFIS, the mosaik framework [14]. Also, existing models and power and usage profiles for the entities in a smart grid (for example electricity grid, photovoltaics, wind energy, private houses, energy stores, electric vehicles [15]) are integrated into this framework.

The smart grid simulation includes public and private consumers as well as energy producers and already considers demand side management between them.

Next to these smart grid entities, we attach a data center simulation, which acts as a normal data center from the smart grid perspective. This means that in a first step, the smart grid simulation framework must not know, if the attached data center is "real" or simulated. It handles the data center as a power consumer, but able to apply demand side management. Therefore, the data center simulation provides information about the power consumption range, described in Sect. 2, to the smart grid.

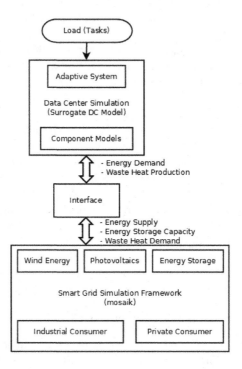

Fig. 1. Simulation architecture of the data center simulation (Surrogate DC Model) and the smart grid simulation framework (mosaik)

It is important to state that both simulation systems are independent of each other. This is an important part of the concept and it leads to a further improvement of the flexibility of the entire simulation system. The simulation concept should be able to answer the following questions:

1. What IT-load profiles can a specific data center operate with?
2. Which modifications of a specific data center architecture can improve the load profile according to a specific desired energy profile?
3. How much time does it take for a fixed data center architecture to transform its energetic state to a another desired state?
4. Up to how much percent can the data center be powered by local renewable energies under the assumption that a desired load profile (from 1.) is operated?

5. How much CO_2 emissions can be saved compared to a conventional energy supply?

Figure 1 shows a diagram of the concept. The smart grid simulation framework mosaik models the energy flow of power producers and consumers, already considering power profiles and usage schedules. The simulation must also be able to create forecasts for the power consumption and power producers.

The interface between the smart grid simulation and the data center simulation contains communication protocols for the following parameters, where the smart grid provides the following information:

- Amount of energy supply available from renewable energy sources in the smart grid for the period of T_{Hnext}
- Amount of storage capacity for power for the period of T_{Hnext}, information about the chronological deferral when discharging the storage (how fast can the storage provide power?)
- Waste heat demand profile for the period of T_{Hnext}

The data center provides the following information:

- Power demand profile for the period of T_{Hnext} and the possible power range including DC_{Pmin} and DC_{Pmax}
- Waste heat production profile for the period of T_{Hnext}

T_{Hnext} defines the duration of the next forecasting period and should be in the range of several hours.

The data center simulation focuses on the key parameters server load (generated by tasks), power consumption and temperature levels, resulting in the generation of waste heat. A Geographic Information System (GIS) will be used to model and simulate external factors that influence these parameters. The simulation system for the data center is represented by the Surrogate DC Model, which is described in detail in the following Sect. 4.

4   Surrogate Data Center Model

The Surrogate DC Model acts as a complete data center to the outside, it is used as a representation of a data center in the smart grid simulation. Internally, it observes the events and actions in the smart grid and adapts itself to these changing conditions. These conditions include changes to the interface parameters listed in Sect. 3, for example a change of the current power that is available from renewable energy sources in the smart grid or the power consumption profiles of the smart grid's consumers. Here, the data center can apply electric load balancing (demand side management).

The Surrogate DC Model has two general options to adjust the power consumption of the simulated data center:

- Short-term reactions: adjust the current virtual machine distribution on the servers by using live-migration.

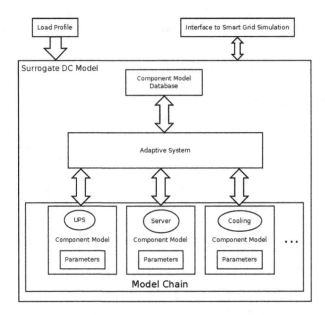

Fig. 2. Details of the Surrogate DC Model that is used to model a data center from the perspective of a smart grid

- Long-term reactions: modify the architecture of the simulated data center.

The details of the Surrogate DC Model are shown in Fig. 2. The input and output communication to the interface to the smart grid simulation matches the parameters listed in Sect. 3. Additionally, the load profile of the tasks that should run in the data center is needed as an input. The Surrogate DC Model uses an internal database with different models for data center components. To adapt itself to a different scenario or to different smart grid conditions, it can exchange its internal simulated components discretely. These component models include several equipment types as well as parameters that can be adjusted to represent a different component behavior.

A key component of this concept is the adaptive system that consists of an artificial intelligence algorithm. It observes the external conditions, controls the current simulation model chain and adjusts the particular models or their parameters.

4.1 Model Architecture

A challenge in this Surrogate DC Model is the development and definition of the architecture of the component models. Different component types need to be exchangeable, but also different data center architectures must be able to be represented by this model chain. For example, a data center may use power storages of the smart grid if they can guarantee an uninterrupted operation and thus it may be able to abstain from the usage of a dedicated Uninterrupted

Power Supply (UPS). Also, thermal energy storages and cold storages locally available may be used by the cooling, leading to architecture modifications of the simulated data center.

From these demands, several requirements for the architecture and the interfaces of the component models arise. Besides the modeling of the energy flow (power and thermal energy), each component must identify its internal type and component category (cooling, power distribution, server, ...) and it must provide information about its internal state. Since the modeling of chronological behavior of the components, as described in Sect. 4.2, is an important simulation aspect, the interfaces will also include timing parameters.

4.2 Modeling Chronological Behavior

One of the key aspects of our simulation concept is the modeling of the temporal behavior of components inside a data center. Figure 3 provides an example of these constellations. For example, the live-migration of virtual machines to

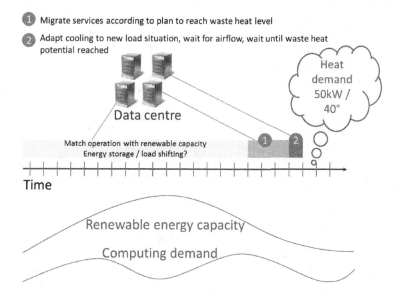

Fig. 3. Timing aspects of data center components (especially cooling) when applying live-migrations

different servers takes a certain amount of time. The target servers will also take some time until they change their temperature level and thus pass their new load situation to the cooling system. Meanwhile, the computing demand as well as the smart grid parameters (renewable energy, power consumption, waste heat demand) underlie deviations. In this example, the aim is now to model these timings so that a data center may be able to shift its tasks, reaching a specific waste heat generation at a certain time. In order to be able to simulate this behavior, fine-granular models of chronological behavior in terms of power consumption and temperature level are needed for each simulated component.

5   Related Work

There has been other research in the areas this paper addresses. The modeling of the thermal behavior of data center components, especially of servers, has been researched before. In [16], the thermal load of processors and micro controllers is considered. [17] handles thermal predictions of processors and combines it with a Dynamic Voltage and Frequency Scaling (DVFS) technique. The thermal modeling of a server rack is arranged in [18]. [19] presents a dynamic model for the temperature and cooling demand of server racks that are enclosed in a hot aisle containment.

General server power models can be found in [13] and [20] while [21] already proposes additional models for racks and cooling units. Energy models for data centers are found in [22] and [7]. Our research partly bases on these results.

In [23], the authors propose the idea to combine a data center with a local power network that includes renewable energy sources. Such a power network is, however, less complex than a smart grid, since it only consists of power producers. The authors also cover the aspect of the intermittency of these power producers. They propose to shift the work load to other data center locations, each profiting from individual energy advantages. A similar approach is covered in [24], including weather conditions at different locations.

[25] proposes a *service request routing* for data centers to distribute the load according to the electric grid in a smart grid.

In [26], the authors present the idea of a carbon-aware data center operation. They propose three key ideas to implement this concept: on-site and off-site renewable energies and Renewable Energy Certificates (REC). In our research, the usage of RECs is, however, not a legitimate concept.

The correlation of power consumption and temperature of server internal coolers is investigated in [27]. As a result, the authors state that it is possible to save power under certain conditions, when the Computer Room Air Conditioning (CRAC) adapts itself to a higher temperature level and the server coolers compensate this by applying a higher rotation frequency. They also model the time that cool air needs to travel from CRAC units to a specific server rack. However, a detailed correlation to server load is not handled.

6   Future Work

In this paper, we introduced our simulation concept and some of the research ideas we intend to follow. Nevertheless, there is a lot of research needed to complete the entire simulation system. A next research topic is the detailed technical definition of the model chain and the interfaces needed for each component model. Also, the technical and programmatic definition of the simulation interface between the smart grid simulation framework mosaik and the Surrogate DC Model will follow. As the Surrogate DC Model needs an artificial intelligence, we need to find and evaluate an appropriate algorithm for this task.

Finally, there are several future thoughts we like to research to extend our simulation concept. Connecting the simulation system to a GIS is a promising idea, since this could allow the usage of spatial weather data. Several cooling concepts rely on weather parameters such as temperature and humidity or other conditions like wind. A detailed modeling of these might improve the simulation results.

7 Conclusion

In this paper, we introduced our simulation concept for data centers in smart grids and, as of our current knowledge, the approach described here is a new methodology in this area. We have motivated the idea of integrating a data center in a smart grid in Sect. 1 with rising energy prices and the upcoming need to use renewable energy sources as much as possible. Connected research listed in Sect. 5 showed that this topic is currently highly relevant to the data center industries. After providing basic information in Sect. 2, we introduced our simulation concept for the combination of smart grid simulations with a specific data center simulation system, with a key aspect on the Surrogate DC Model. This model will adapt its internal structure and the internal components to a data center architecture that provides optimal synergy effects according to the particular smart grid location. Our work is still in concept and a lot of future research is still to do, but we expect this approach to be very promising.

Acknowledgements. This scientific work is funded by the German Federal Ministry of Economics and Technology (BMWi) under grant no. 01ME11048 (project AC4DC - Adaptive Computing for green Data Centers).

References

1. Fettweis, G., Zimmermann, E.: ICT Energy Consumption Trends and Challenges. In: The 11th International Symposium on Wireless Personal Multimedia Communications (2008)
2. Meeker, M.: Internet Trends. Technical Report, D10 Conference (2012)
3. Fisa, M.G.: European Perspectives in Addressing Sustainability in Data Centres (In Context, in Particular, of Urban Environments). Technical Report, Smart Cities and Sustainability Directorate-General Communications Networks, Content and Technology European Commission (2012)
4. Barham, P., Dragovic, B., Fraser, K., Hand, S., Harris, T., Ho, A., Neugebauer, R., Pratt, I., Warfield, A.: Xen and the Art of Virtualization. In: Proceedings of the Nineteenth ACM Symposium on Operating Systems Principles, pp. 164–177. ACM, New York (2003)

5. Hoyer, M., Schroeder, K., Schlitt, D., Nebel, W.: Proactive Dynamic Resource Management in Virtualized Data Centers. In: Proceedings of the 2nd International Conference on Energy-Efficient Computing and Networking, pp. 11–20. ACM, New York (2011)
6. Kusic, D., Kephart, J.O., Hanson, J.E., Kandasamy, N., Jiang, G.: Power and Performance Management of Virtualized Computing Environments via Lookahead Control. In: International Conference on Autonomic Computing, pp. 3–12. IEEE Computer Society, Washington (2008)
7. Mukherjee, T., Banerjee, A., Varsamopoulos, G., Gupta, S.K.S., Rungta, S.: Spatio-temporal Thermal-aware Job Scheduling to Minimize Energy Consumption in Virtualized Heterogeneous Data Centers. In: Computer Networks, Special Issue on Resource Management in Heterogeneous Data Centers, vol. 53(17), pp. 2888–2904. Elsevier North-Holland, Inc., New York (2009)
8. Beloglazov, A., Buyya, R.: Adaptive Threshold-based Approach for Energy-efficient Consolidation of Virtual Machines in Cloud Data Centers. In: Proceedings of the 8th International Workshop on Middleware for Grids, Clouds and e-Science, pp. 4:1-4:6. ACM, New York (2010)
9. Miller, R.: Data Centers That Recycle Waste Heat. Technical Report, datacenter knowledge (2010)
10. Denholm, P., Ela, E., Kirby, B., Milligan, M.: The Role of Energy Storage with Renewable Electricity Generation. Technical Report, NREL/TP-6A2-47187 (2010)
11. Grid, T.G.: Carbon Usage Effectiveness (CUE): A Green Grid Data Center Sustainability Metric. Technical Report (2010)
12. Grid, T.G.: The Green Grid Data Center Power Efficiency Metrics: PUE and DCiE. Technical Report (2007)
13. Janacek, S., Schroeder, K., Schomaker, G., Nebel, W., Rueschen, M., Pistoor, G.: Modeling and Approaching a Cost Transparent, Specific Data Center Power Consumption. In: 2012 International Conference on Energy Aware Computing, pp. 68–73. IEEE, New York (2012)
14. Schuette, S., Scherfke, S., Troeschel, T.: Mosaik: A Framework for Modular Simulation of Active Components in Smart Grids. In: IEEE First International Workshop on Smart Grid Modeling and Simulation (SGMS), pp. 55–60. IEEE, New York (2011)
15. Schuette, S., Sonnenschein, M.: Mosaik - Scalable Smart Grid Scenario Specification. In: Proceedings of the 2012 Winter Simulation Conference, pp. 1–12. IEEE, New York (2012)
16. Wu, W., Jin, L., Yang, J., Liu, P., Tan, S.: Efficient Power Modeling and Software Thermal Sensing for Runtime Temperature Monitoring. ACM Transactions on Design Automation of Electronic Systems 12(3), 25:1-25:29 (2008)
17. Cochran, R., Reda, S.: Consistent Runtime Thermal Prediction and Control Through Workload Phase Detection. In: Proceedings of the 47th Design Automation Conference, pp. 62–67. ACM, New York (2010)
18. Jeonghwan, C., Youngjae, K.A., Jelena, S., Qian, W., Joonwon, L.: Modeling and Managing Thermal Profiles of Rack-mounted Servers with ThermoStat. In: Proceedings of HPCA, pp. 205–215. IEEE, New York (2007)
19. Zhou, R., Wang, Z., Bash, C.E., McReynolds, A.: Modeling and Control for Cooling Management of Data Centers With Hot Aisle Containment. In: ASME Conference Proceedings, pp. 739–746. ASME, New York (2011)
20. Pedram, M., Hwang, I.: Power and Performance Modeling in a Virtualized Server System. In: Proceedings of the 2010 39th International Conference on Parallel Processing Workshops, pp. 520–526 (2010)

21. Pakbaznia, E., Pedram, M.: Minimizing Data Center Cooling and Server Power Costs. In: Proceedings of the 14th ACM/IEEE International Symposium on Low Power Electronics and Design, pp. 145–150. ACM, New York (2009)
22. Abbasi, Z., Varsamopoulos, G., Gupta, S.K.S.: Thermal Aware Server Provisioning and Workload Distribution for Internet Data Centers. In: Proceedings of the 19th ACM International Symposium on High Performance Distributed Computing, pp. 130–141. ACM, New York (2010)
23. Ghamkhari, M., Mohsenian-Rad, H.: Optimal Integration of Renewable Energy Resources in Data Centers with Behind-the-Meter Renewable Generator. In: IEEE International Conference on Communications (ICC), pp. 3340–3344. IEEE, New York (2012)
24. Zhang, Y., Wang, Y., Wang, X.: GreenWare: Greening Cloud-Scale Data Centers to Maximize the Use of Renewable Energy. In: Kon, F., Kermarrec, A.-M. (eds.) Middleware 2011. LNCS, vol. 7049, pp. 143–164. Springer, Heidelberg (2011)
25. Mohsenian-Rad, H., Leon-Garcia, A.: Coordination of Cloud Computing and Smart Power Grids. In: Proceedings of IEEE Smart Grid Communications Conference, pp. 368-372. IEEE, New York (2010)
26. Ren, C., Wang, D., Urgaonkar, B., Sivasubramaniam, A.: Carbon-Aware Energy Capacity Planning for Datacenters. In: IEEE 20th International Symposium on Modeling, Analysis Simulation of Computer and Telecommunication Systems, pp. 391–400. IEEE, New York (2012)
27. Sungkap, Y., Lee, H.H.S.: SimWare: A Holistic Warehouse-Scale Computer Simulator. Computer 45(9), 48–55 (2012)

Author Index